THE DA VINCI DECODE

THE DA VINCI DECODE

IS CHRISTIANITY "THE GREATEST COVER-UP IN HUMAN HISTORY"?

GRENVILLE KENT
PHILIP RODIONOFF

SIGNS
PUBLISHING
COMPANY

Printed and published by
SIGNS PUBLISHING COMPANY
Victoria, Australia

Page references to *The Da Vinci Code* are to the 2004 Corgi edition. The cover quotation is from page 336.

This book refers to dates by BC and AD because these are more commonly understood than BCE and CE.

Additional copies of this book are available by visiting

www.thedavincidecode.net

Edited by Nathan Brown and Graeme H Brown

Designed by Shane Winfield

Cover illustration by Dan North

Cover design by Shane Winfield

Cryptex photo by iStockphoto

Typeset in 11/14 Bembo

ISBN 1 876010 90 8

DEDICATION

GK: To the octopus goalie and our team, the dancing winger, the lightning striker and the ravenous fullback, with love from the midfield.

"Wisdom is justified by all her children" (Luke 7:35, NKJV).

And to Mim and Saba, with thanks and love.

PR: To my parents, Leonard and Helen Rodionoff, for your inspiration, mentoring and love.

The authors wish to thank
Aaron Bartlett; Hannah Bath; Nathan Brown;
Graeme Christian; Dr Alex Currie; James Etwell;
Eliezer Gonzalez; Neroli Hills-Perry; Carla Kent;
Gary Kent; Michelle Mulligan; Dan North;
Dr Sven Ostring; Dr Paul Petersen; Anne-Marie Raymond;
David Riley; Amanda Rodionoff; Paul Rodionoff;
Hans and Herta von Stiegel; Dr Clinton Wahlen;
Jasmine Wallace; Students at Wesley Institute

CONTENTS

Chapter 1

THE COVER-UP?

*T*he *Da Vinci Code* is a blockbuster. First released in 2003, Dan Brown's novel has sold more than 40 million copies in 42 languages, and is now also a major Hollywood film. It's been called a "code-breaking, exhilarating, brainy thriller" (*New York Times*) and the "biggest selling adult . . . fiction book of all time" (*Daily Telegraph*).

Some question its literary merit, but many more have been gripped by the plot twists and fast-paced storytelling. It seems that any plane, train or suburban bus will include a reader or two, enthralled by their paperback copy. The characters are appealing, from the hunky Professor Robert Langdon, the stunning and brilliant Sophie and her lovable genius grandfather, through to the eccentric and devious Sir Leigh Teabing and Silas the murdering psycho-monk, who still somehow attracts our sympathy.

The Da Vinci Code has inspired many imitators, plus more than 20 major books and documentary films with historians and other specialists debunking many of its historical claims.

Yet people are taking *The Da Vinci Code* seriously, accepting the theories promoted by its characters. One overhears commuters making comments like, "How can you be a Christian after reading *The Da Vinci Code*? It disproves the whole thing." Even some Christians are wondering whether the Bible is fiction and the novel is fact.

Why is *The Da Vinci Code* so popular?
Aside from being a gripping story, *The Da Vinci Code* raises issues

relevant to contemporary culture.

1. It questions organised religion.

Questioning the church is a popular indoor sport in today's increasingly secular society. And not without reason. For example, James Rudin of Religious News Service, in an article on the top 10 religion stories of 2005, included the following comment: "The Roman Catholic Church, especially in the US and Ireland, suffered from a continuing sexual abuse scandal involving priests. The staggering financial costs of payments to victims bankrupted some dioceses." Other churches have faced greedy, sleazy TV evangelists and other scandals.

In Brown's novel, Sir Leigh Teabing scores that point, claiming that people "look at Church scandals and ask, who *are* these men who claim to speak the truth about Christ and yet lie to cover up the sexual abuse of children by their own priests?"[1]

Unfortunately, it's a fair comment. We humbly admit many Christian leaders have acted in unchristian or un-Christlike ways. Christian academic Greg Clarke goes further with one surprising and powerful word: *sorry*. In a book arguing with many of Brown's historical theories, Clarke shows his fair-mindedness by saying, "Christians are definitely guilty of some of the claims of this novel, and I for one am sorry about it."[2] He admits that "if the Church can hide such heinous sins within its ranks," then it is clear why people "would be attracted to the idea that the Church was hiding a secret as big as the identity of Jesus and Mary Magdalene. When trust has been betrayed, then anything seems possible."

Clarke admits the church has at times acted like a "bully." He balances this by saying most priests (and vicars and pastors) are not corrupt, and most people's experience with church is positive, but he can see why "post-Christians" might doubt the church.[3] And so he says, "Sorry . . . that the Church has sometimes hidden the truth from people," and sorry "for not presenting the truth as we understand it in an exciting, attractive and believable way. . . . Sorry for being boring. . . . Christians can make Christianity seem mundane, all about rules, or all about denying yourself pleasures. If we do, we present a distorted view of Christianity."

Even Jesus criticised religious organisations. He commented to some priests 2000 years ago: "I tell you the truth, the tax collectors and the prostitutes are entering the kingdom of God ahead of you" (Matthew 21:31). Imagine Jesus looking religious leaders in the eye and telling them that the very people they looked down upon were actually further along the path to heaven than they were. Jesus told a group of priests that they slammed the door of heaven in people's faces and were not going in themselves (see Matthew 23:13). No wonder they crucified Him. He told the truth about religious corruption in His day and age.

So it's hardly surprising today that there are examples of religious organisations acting terribly, even while mouthing nice words. Jesus warned about that.

In fairness, churches also motivate the haves to give to the have-nots. They run charities and soup kitchens and hospitals, and educate the poor and contribute millions of hours of volunteer work each year to people who are old, sick, lonely and marginalised. They serve, inspired by the life and words of Jesus Christ.

But let's not back away from the glaring examples of church greed, corruption and abuse from people who are preaching and talking down to others.

Perhaps the church is God's most serious image problem.

No wonder criticism of the church gets people's attention. And what better way to wipe the smug smile off Christians' faces than to prove the whole story is a myth! Except that, as we'll see, Brown doesn't manage to prove it.

2. People love exposing a cover-up.

Many of us seem to be quite ready to believe big business and big government are trying to pull the wool over our eyes, and we love to see the truth told. For many, the church is just one more multinational organisation with its own agendas, so why not debunk it as well?

And there is some merit in that. If there is corruption in the church, exposing it can lead to change, so that the good that is in Christianity is easier to find.

3. The novel promotes a fashionable spirituality.

Greg Clarke says he can understand why *The Da Vinci Code* is such an attractive alternative. It "offers a view of religion that can seem more human, more in contact with the real world, more about relationships and experiences and love and sex and celebration."[4]

Brown's fictional hero, Professor Robert Langdon, argues that traditional Christianity is a perversion of the original faith, which was much less hung-up about sex, and also much more respectful of women. Historically, he has a point. Churches have often kept women in second place to men, while Jesus did not teach or practise such sexism. But Brown is wrong in claiming that the earliest Christians worshipped women as goddesses.

The book ends up trying to give Christianity a makeover and make it look more like New Age spirituality. But Christianity at its best does not need such retouching. Like a classic painting, it sometimes needs centuries of grimy dogma carefully removed so the original colours can be seen. As Clarke claims, real Christianity is "nothing short of astounding. We think [Jesus] is the key to understanding the purpose of life. We think He opens up the opportunity for freedom, hope and mercy for all people who believe in Him. And we believe that He rose from the grave and in doing so demonstrated His power over the things we fear most. We're excited by these spiritual ideas."[5]

4. The Da Vinci Code sounds democratic about spiritual truth.

Many people in Western society are suspicious of authority figures and would identify with Sophie's grandfather when he says, "The Church should not be allowed to tell us what notions we can and can't entertain."[6] (Jesus probably would too—He emphasised individual accountability.)

Most of us are wary of dogma. If someone claims to have spiritual truth others do not have, most Westerners would find them arrogant and small-minded. In fact we are so keen that people of all races and beliefs must get on in our cosmopolitan cities—which is of course good—that we almost want to avoid discussions about the truth or untruth of beliefs. We play word games, saying things like, "X is true for you, but not for me." But if one person says, "Jesus really died and resurrected," and someone else says, "Jesus' resurrection was a myth," can they both be right? And doesn't real citizenship require the ability to get along with those with whom we disagree?

Dr Michael Green agrees that this tendency is evidenced by the popularity of *The Da Vinci Code*. He lightheartedly speaks for Western audiences:

"Down with the Vatican and all its corruption and deception! Down with the Gospels and the deity of Christ. Down with the authoritarianism that has marked a male-dominated church. Let's replace it with an all-inclusive neo-paganism, where the sacred feminine comes into its own, where nobody is told what to believe, where all religions are much the same, and where nature worship with full sexual permissiveness is on the agenda. All of this is very attractive in today's society."[7]

Yet Green warns that "Brown's claim to factual accuracy, playing on the contemporary tendency to confuse fact with fiction," makes the book potentially deceptive, especially because most people know so little about original Christianity.

"America is a Jesus-haunted culture," says Professor Ben Witherington III, "but at the same time, it's a biblically illiterate culture. When you have that odd combination, almost anything can pass for knowledge of the historical Jesus."[8]

Claims against Christianity

Like many good stories, *The Da Vinci Code* is not just a good story. The book makes some big truth-claims, and sets out to expose what it describes as "the greatest cover-up in human history"[9]—within Christianity itself. It makes the following radical claims about the Christian faith:

▶ that Jesus Christ was not God in human form, but only human—a "mortal prophet";[10]

▶ that history was rewritten in 325 AD when the Roman emperor Constantine and the church Council of Nicaea voted to upgrade Jesus to God status so as to strengthen their own power;[11]

▶ that Mary Magdalene was divine, but that sexist churchmen could not handle that truth;[12]

▶ that Jesus and Mary were married, and that their descendants have included the kings of France and certain people still alive in Europe;[13]

▶ that Roman Catholic Church leaders know the truth but have used violence and terror tactics to cover it up and maintain church power.[14]

These are huge claims, and the website <catholic.com> gets right to the point: "If the book's claims were true, then all forms of Christianity would be false (except perhaps for Gnostic/feminist versions focusing on Mary Magdalene instead of Jesus)."

This theory has been proposed before, in a 1982 book *The Holy Blood and the Holy Grail* by Michael Baigent, Richard Leigh and Henry Lincoln. (Codebreakers will notice that the novel's character Leigh Teabing is named after the surnames of the first two authors, with the letters of Baigent rearranged into Teabing. Despite that credit, these two authors have tried suing Brown for copying their material—unsuccessfully, though Brown admits using their book among many others.) And there have been other New Age authors who allege similar conspiracies by secret societies, although they are considered a quirky fringe, not within the mainstream of serious historians.

Yet the novel is extremely influential. *Time* magazine recently listed Brown among the 100 most influential people in the world. So let's take a closer look at the novel's claims, using independent historical sources.

How factual is it?

At a villa outside Paris, the character Leigh Teabing expounds these theories to Sophie and Langdon. He says "the early Church" hijacked Jesus Christ's "human message, surrounding it in an impenetrable cloak of divinity." He says Jesus existed and "was indeed a great and powerful man. . . . Nobody is saying Christ was a fraud, or denying that He walked the earth and inspired millions to better lives." But "Constantine upgraded Jesus" from man to God almost four centuries *after* Jesus' death, and so "thousands of documents already existed chronicling His life as a *mortal* man." "Constantine commissioned and financed a new Bible, which omitted those gospels that spoke of Christ's *human* traits and embellished those gospels that made Him godlike. The earlier gospels were outlawed, gathered up and burned."[15]

These few lines give us much to consider:

1. Teabing (or Brown) accepts that Jesus was a historical figure who walked the earth and inspired millions. No serious historian doubts that Jesus of Nazareth was a historical figure. As we'll see, various independent Roman historians found Jesus strange or annoying, but they stated the fact that He lived, and was a religious teacher believed by His followers to be God; and official Jewish historical

sources criticise Him and do not accept He was the Messiah—but they acknowledge that He really existed in history.

2. Teabing claims Jesus was human and mortal, as recorded in many Gospels. (A Gospel is a biography of Jesus, written by an eyewitness or compiled from eyewitness testimony. The word originally meant "good news" and the writers thought God becoming human was great news.) But Teabing claims any Gospels describing Christ's human traits were omitted, outlawed, gathered up and burned.

But the accepted Gospels—Matthew, Mark, Luke and John, as found in the Bible at the beginning of the New Testament—often show Jesus doing very human things. At times He was tired, hungry, sad, tempted, rejected by His hometown crowd, His power limited, and growing in wisdom.[16] His real humanity is emphasised in the Gospels recognised by every Christian church.

Christians have always taught that Jesus was human, though God as well. That may seem a huge contradiction, and Christians since earliest times have found it a mind-boggling "mystery," but a beautiful demonstration of God's sympathy with the human race.

God became human, while of course also remaining God. Many people may imagine God as a "stern judge," a "mighty storm" or a "triumphant warrior"—but who would think of God as "a slave hanging on a cross"? Yet this is how Jesus is presented in a Christian poem recorded in 62-63 AD,[17] celebrating the self-giving love and humility of God.

And other books in the New Testament are very hard line about the fact that God became a real human. The rabbi-turned-Christian, Paul, wrote, "See to it that no-one takes you captive through hollow and deceptive philosophy. . . . For in Christ all the fullness of the Deity lives in bodily form" (Colossians 2:8, 9).

So Brown is wrong to say that Gospels showing a human Jesus were burned. They were treasured—and still are.

3. Teabing's theory that Gospels were burned is an argument from silence. He gives no historical evidence for the claim. We have records of Constantine in 325 AD ordering the burning of documents by an unorthodox writer named Arius, but they were

certainly not Gospels. The burning of Gospels is total imagination. Imagination is why we pay novelists so well, but imagination is not to be taken as serious history or religion.

Teabing continues: "Fortunately for historians . . . some of the gospels that Constantine attempted to eradicate managed to survive. The Dead Sea Scrolls were found in the 1950s hidden in a cave near Qumran in the Judaean desert. And, of course, the Coptic Scrolls in 1945 at Nag Hammadi. In addition to telling the true Grail story, these documents speak of Christ's ministry in very human terms. Of course, the Vatican, in keeping with their tradition of misinformation, tried very hard to suppress the release of these scrolls. And why wouldn't they? The scrolls highlight glaring historical discrepancies and fabrications, clearly confirming that the modern Bible was compiled and edited by men who possessed a political agenda—to promote the divinity of the man Jesus Christ and use His influence to solidify their own power base."[18]

Another list of big claims for us to consider:

4. Teabing lists the Dead Sea Scrolls as "gospels"—books about Jesus. This is a serious mistake in research. The Dead Sea Scrolls are Jewish books, not Christian. You can buy a translated copy of the scrolls at major bookshops, and you'll see they contain most of the Hebrew Bible (also called the Old Testament), as well as writings from a conservative, desert-dwelling Jewish community. Teabing calls them "the earliest Christian records,"[19] but they're Jewish and pre-Christian. Most of the copies date from at least 100 years before Christ. This is stated in any encyclopedia and should have come up in Brown's research. He claims on the "Fact" page that "all descriptions of artwork, architecture, documents and secret rituals in this novel are accurate."

5. What about the discovery at Nag Hammadi in 1945?[20] They were not actually "scrolls," as Teabing says, but a collection of leather-bound books, written in Coptic, an ancient Egyptian language. Two farmers found them by accident and one, named Muhammed Ali (a common Muslim name), carried them back to the Egyptian town of Nag Hammadi.

Scholars found them to be papyrus books from the 4th century, some 300 years after Christ. They are copies of documents written in Greek before 250 AD. "The official translator of the Nag Hammadi library puts the date of the Gospel of Philip at 250 AD. The earliest date that has ever been suggested is 175 AD."[21] Even that date was some 144 years after Jesus' death, so there were no eyewitnesses of Jesus involved in the writing process.

The 13 books contained 45 different titles, most previously unknown, including a few that were called "gospels": the Gospel of Truth, The Gospel of Thomas and the Gospel of Philip. The rest of the books were mystical speculations.[22]

Even a quick read of these "gospels" reveals a very different Jesus, who does not blink or leave footprints, and only appears human if you don't look too closely. So much for Teabing's claim that they show Jesus in "very human terms." And they certainly do not show up "glaring historical discrepancies," because they're not historical in nature, but mystical.

Neither do these "gospels" have any mention of the Holy Grail, the obsession of various characters in *The Da Vinci Code*. Traditional stories see the Grail as the cup Christ used during the Last Supper, and claim that finding it would bring untold blessing. *The Da Vinci Code* portrays the Grail as Mary herself. But this is certainly not drawn from these documents.

There are Gnostic gospels other than those found at Nag Hammadi. For example, the Gospel of Mary, to which Teabing refers, was discovered in Cairo in 1896.

But there has been no cover-up. The early church fathers quoted Gnostic writers in their own writings and argued against them publicly, using free speech rather than trying to hush them up. And Christian scholars have welcomed the recent finds as a fascinating insight into Gnosticism, a religion opposed by some of the later New Testament books.[23]

6. What about Teabing's (or Brown's) statement that "thousands of documents" before 325 AD chronicled Jesus' life as an ordinary man rather than God, and that no-one before 325 AD believed Jesus was God?

There are two lines of evidence. At this stage, we're not trying to prove Jesus was God; we're just trying to show that

What are the Gnostic "gospels"?

The term Gnostic means "a knowing one." Gnostics believed they were enlightened with secret truth.

An esoteric religion that came in many different forms, Gnosticism was based on the idea that the material world was evil, while the spiritual realm was good. It taught human beings were made of a soul (which was good) and a body (which was evil or, at best, ignorant and blundering). They believed there was a low-grade god who made the earth but that the Supreme Being had made our souls and wanted to enlighten us.

You can imagine what a Gnostic made of Jesus. He was a messenger from the Supreme Being to enlighten our souls. But He didn't really take a human body (because bodies are evil). He only seemed to be in a body. And He didn't really die (because souls cannot die).

This is the view expressed in these Gnostic "gospels." Christians took major issue with Gnostic beliefs. Christians:

◆ know of only one God (in three Persons) who is good and perfect, not some lesser god.

◆ believe this God is the Creator of everything, and that God called the physical world "good" (seven times in the Creation story of Genesis 1). So the human body is not evil.

◆ believe the human body and the whole natural world are affected by sin (going against God's plan), but God still wants to redeem and restore humans and the natural world. In heaven both people and nature will be perfect again.

◆ believe Jesus really was God in human flesh, a human body.

◆ believe Jesus lived without sinning, and died to take away the guilt of anyone who believes in Him, and thus to give them eternal life. This is a major teaching of Christianity. And Christians understand we can come to believe this by hearing good eyewitness evidence (see Romans 10:17; 1 John 1:3; 2 Peter 1:16-21), not just by some flash of enlightenment (which may be very subjective).

Early Christian writers like Irenaeus, Tertullian and Hippolytus argued against Gnosticism, calling it pagan, based on the ideas of the Greek philosopher Plato. The apostle John, who was the youngest of Jesus' disciples and lived until 97 AD, saw an early form of Gnosticism and argued against it, especially defending the idea of Jesus as God in human flesh (see 1 John 4:1-3; 2 John 7).

So in summary:

(a) The Gnostic "gospels" were Gnostic, not Christian. Gnostics and Christians were from very different religions, and in constant debate.

(b) If they were written from 150 to 250 AD, then they were not written by eyewitnesses to Jesus' life. They may claim to be written by Thomas or Philip, but those disciples were long dead by the time these gospels were written.

Nicky Gumbel puts it well: "The Nag Hammadi manuscripts are not really Gospels at all. The Gnostic 'gospels' are non-historical, and even anti-historical, with little narrative or sense of chronology. They were written generations after the facts while claiming direct, secret knowledge about them."[24]

So why does Brown like these "gospels"? One reason is that he believes in gender equality and thinks these gospels are pro-women. But consider how The Gospel of Thomas ends:

Simon Peter said, "Let Mary leave us, for women are not worthy of Life."

Jesus said, "I myself shall lead her in order to make her male, so that she too may become a living spirit resembling you males. For every woman who will make herself male will enter the Kingdom of Heaven" (Saying 114).

This bizarrely sexist comment doesn't fit Brown's theory of Jesus as the original feminist or Mary as the "sacred feminine." So even these "gospels" don't support his theory unless quoted selectively.

early Christians believed Jesus was God from the very first, long before 325 AD. Here's the evidence:

(a) Christian writers

Writing in the second and third centuries, the early church leaders or "fathers" clearly expressed the belief that Jesus is God. Some would argue that the church could have forged this evidence after they changed the story, but is it likely that they could plant these quotes in known books when the authors came from various different countries, and when copies existed in many different places?

(b) Evidence from Roman history

Independent Roman historians, whose works are key texts in ancient history to this day, also record that the early Christians believed Jesus was God in the flesh. This is the strongest evidence. Even if Constantine could burn gospels, he couldn't change the writings of historians whose works were widely spread and well accepted by that time.

An example: Plinius Secundus (or Pliny the Younger) was the Roman governor of Bithynia in 112 AD. He wrote to the emperor Trajan reporting that he had been going out of his way to kill Christians, and asking the emperor whether he should keep hunting them down. Obviously, he was not biased in favour of Christians! Pliny reports their "crime": "they were in the habit of meeting on a certain fixed day before it was light, when they sang in alternate verse a hymn to Christ as to a God, and bound themselves to a solemn oath, not to do any wicked

The "church fathers" claim Jesus as God

- ◆ c 110 AD—Ignatius of Antioch (in Syria): "For our God, Jesus Christ, was conceived by Mary in accord with God's plan: of the seed of David, it is true, but also of the Holy Spirit" (*Letter to the Ephesians*, 18:2).
- ◆ c 170 AD—Tatian the Syrian: "We are not playing the fool, you Greeks, nor do we talk nonsense, when we report that God was born in the form of a man" (*Address to the Greeks*, 21).
- ◆ c 190 AD—Clement of Alexandria (in Egypt): "The Word, then, the Christ, is the cause both of our ancient beginning—for he was in God—and of our wellbeing. And now this same Word has appeared as man. He alone is both God and man, and the source of all our good things" (*Exhortation to the Greeks*, 1:7:1).
- ◆ c 210 AD—Tertullian of Carthage (in North Africa): "God alone is without sin. The only man who is without sin is Christ; for Christ is also God" (*The Soul*, 41:3).
- ◆ c 225 AD—Origen: "Although he was God, he took flesh; and having been made man, he remained what he was: God" (*The Fundamental Doctrines*, 1:0:4).

See www.catholic.com/library/cracking_da_vinci_code.asp

deeds, but never to commit any fraud, theft, adultery, never to falsify their word" (*Epistles* X, 26).

Christians are still doing those things, worshipping Christ as God. The belief has not changed in nearly 2000 years.

So apart from the Bible, which includes a number of first-century writers who obviously believed Jesus was God, there is strong evidence the earliest Christians believed Jesus was God in human flesh—long before Constantine in 325 AD.

A+ for creative writing, F for history

While *The Da Vinci Code* is an enjoyable novel, it seems Brown has either not done his historical homework or has not let the facts stand in the way of a good story. Genuine academic historians have a hard time taking many of the claims seriously.

Perhaps Brown has become a little sick of hearing this, because he asks on his website <danbrown.com>: "How historically accurate is history itself?" This is an interesting defensive tactic, because if he shoots down history itself, he shoots down his own claim to have the real history. It sounds like someone trying to silence the critique of the many historians who've spoken up.

Bottom line: great story, dodgy history. As a recent *Time* magazine article put it, "Strictly speaking, the novel is heretical. It's perhaps worth noting that one of the very few books to sell more copies than *The Da Vinci Code* in the past two years is the Bible."[25]

Brown has asked some fascinating questions about Jesus, and is looking for a spirituality free from dogma, arrogance about truth, hypocrisy, unreasonable laws and sexism. The Jesus of the New Testament would probably agree with many of those aims, as we'll see in later chapters of this book.

Chapter 2

JESUS: MORTAL PROPHET OR SON OF GOD?

J esus of Nazareth is one of the most controversial figures of history, and *The Da Vinci Code* is just the latest chapter in a 2000-year–old discussion.

Through his character Leigh Teabing, Brown's novel argues that Jesus was just a human until the Roman emperor Constantine and a church council in 325 AD declared that He was a god:

- ▶ ". . . until that moment in history, Jesus was viewed by His followers as a mortal prophet . . . a great and powerful man, but a man nonetheless. A mortal."[1]
- ▶ "Jesus' establishment as 'the Son of God' was officially proposed and voted on by the Council of Nicaea. [And it was] a relatively close vote at that."[2]
- ▶ ". . . almost everything our fathers taught us about Christ is false."[3]

As we have seen, the earliest Christians actually did believe Jesus was God in human flesh, as did many Christian writers before 325 AD. But were they dreaming? Were they deluded by sincere faith and religious showmanship? Did they make their claims to make money or achieve stardom? Or could it be that they had strong evidence that Jesus was much more than a great human teacher?

The major reason the first Christians had for believing Jesus' divinity was that they believed He died and then days later came back to life.

At this point, Christianity puts its credibility on the line. The Christian teacher Paul, writing in about 54 AD,[4] put it this way: "If Christ has not been raised, our preaching is useless and so is your faith. More than that, we are then found to be false witnesses about God, for we have testified about God that He raised Christ from the dead. . . . And if Christ has not been raised, your faith is futile; you are still in your sins . . . [and] we [Christians] are to be pitied more than all men. But Christ has indeed been raised from the dead" (1 Corinthians 15:14-20).

This is a huge claim—and a dangerous thing to put in writing. Paul hangs the whole credibility of the Christian faith on Jesus rising from the dead. If that has not happened in actual history, then Christianity is a useless fake.

Many religions keep their truth-claims vague, so they are hard to disprove. If you could discredit the history of their founders or gods, they would probably smile patiently and say it doesn't matter because the truly enlightened will not need objective verification. Some even see the quest for evidence as anti-faith: you are either enlightened to the awareness or you are not, and better luck next lifetime. But if you can't disprove religion, can you really prove it? Christianity wants rational belief—it wants to appeal to the head as well as the heart. It offers mystical experience, but also aims to be believable, and makes verifiable statements about the real world.

Hanging the whole faith on the resurrection of Jesus would be a disastrous move if there was no evidence. The early Christians must have been very confident of their facts. So let's explore some of this evidence.

1. Jesus was a real figure of history

It would be rather weak to cite only Christian sources for the historical reality of Jesus. At least 15 non-Christian sources, dating from the first and second centuries, mention Jesus as a historical figure.[5] Let's examine some of these. (And you can check these references in any good encyclopedia.)

In the British Museum is a fascinating manuscript alluding to Jesus. It was written soon after 73 AD by a Syrian named Mara Bar-Serapion to his son, Serapion. The father was in prison, but wrote to encourage his son to keep pursuing wisdom, and showed that even the best and wisest men suffered misfortune. He asks: "What advantage did the Athenians

Roman historians:

Tacitus

Cornelius Tacitus (born c 52 AD) is "probably the greatest historian . . . who wrote in the Latin language."[6]

In his 18-volume *Annals,* of about 105 AD, Tacitus writes about Nero being blamed for starting the fire in Rome: "Hence to suppress the rumour, he falsely charged with the guilt, and punished with the most exquisite tortures, the persons commonly called Christians, who were hated for their enormities [crimes]. Christus, the founder of the name, was put to death by Pontius Pilate, procurator of Judea in the reign of Tiberias" (*Annals,* XV, 44).

This independently confirms that Jesus was executed by Pontius Pilate, as recorded in the Gospels (see Matthew 27; Mark 15; Luke 23; John 18, 19).

Lucian

Lucian of Samosata (born 120 AD) was a Greek satirist who made jokes at the expense of Christians.[7] He told his readers to pretend to be Christians when visiting foreign cities, so as to get free food and accommodation from gullible Christians. Lucian called Jesus "the man who was crucified in Palestine because he introduced this new cult to the world." He says of Christians: "The poor wretches have convinced themselves, first and foremost, that they are going to be immortal and live for all time, in consequence of which they despise death and even willingly give themselves into custody; most of them. Furthermore, their first lawgiver persuaded them that they are all brothers of one another." He describes them as "worshipping that crucified sophist himself and living under his laws."[8]

Lucian saw Christians as easy targets, and calls Jesus a sophist, "a teacher" of dubious reasoning[9] but at least Lucian records that He lived—and that He was crucified, and that after His crucifixion people worshipped Him in the place of Greek gods and lived under His laws, awaiting immortality. If a Christian wrote that, you might claim bias. But Lucian was not trying to do Christians a favour, yet he did. We almost feel like inviting him to dinner.

Josephus

Flavius Josephus (born 37 AD) was a Jew and commander of the Jewish forces in Galilee, but was captured by the Romans and penned his histories.

He wrote in the early second century:

"At this time there was a wise man called Jesus, and his conduct was good, and he was known to be virtuous. And many people from among the Jews and other nations became his disciples. Pilate condemned him to be crucified and to die. And those who had become his disciples did not abandon their discipleship. They reported that he had appeared to them three days after his crucifixion and that he was alive. Accordingly, he was perhaps the Messiah concerning whom the prophets have recounted wonders."[10]

Josephus elsewhere writes of "Jesus the so-called Christ" (*Antiquities* XX, 9:1). This is strong confirmation. Josephus is not a Christian, but records the history of Jesus being:

- executed on a cross by Pilate
- reported to appear alive three days later
- "perhaps the Messiah" (Josephus is a Jew, not a Christian, but does not write off the idea of Jesus being the Messiah)
- predicted by ancient prophets (see Chapter 3 of this book).

Plinius Secundus (or Pliny the Younger) was discussed in the previous chapter.

gain from putting Socrates to death? Famine and plague came upon them. . . . What advantage did the men of Samos gain from burning Pythagoras? In a moment their land was covered with sand. What advantage did the Jews gain from killing their wise King? It was just after that that their kingdom was abolished. God justly avenged these three wise men."[11] This Syrian man obviously thought Jesus was as historical as Pythagoras or Socrates.

When a Christian like Tertullian, the legal mind of Carthage, defended Christianity in 197 AD before the Roman authorities, he could mention the communication between the governor Pontius Pilate and the emperor Tiberius—and no Roman doubted his history. Tertullian wrote:

Tiberius accordingly, in whose days the Christian name made its entry into the world, having himself received intelligence from Palestine of events which had clearly shown the truth of Christ's divinity, brought the matter before the Senate, with his own decision in favour of Christ. The Senate, because it had not given the approval itself, rejected his proposal. Caesar held to his opinion, threatening wrath against all the accusers of the Christians (*Apology*, V, 2).

So Jesus was known to Roman history.

Jewish history

The Jewish Talmuds (major books of Jewish law and learning) also mention Jesus. A reference in the Babylonian Talmud fits exactly with the Bible's account of Jesus hanging on the cross just before the Jewish feast of Passover: "On the eve of Passover they hanged Yeshu (of Nazareth) . . . in that he hath practised sorcery and beguiled and led astray Israel" (*Babylonian Sanhedrin*, 43a). Calling Him a sorcerer suggests magical or miraculous powers—and the Gospels also record Jesus being accused of sorcery by some Jewish leaders (see Matthew 12:24; Mark 3:22).

The Talmud calls Him "Ben Pandera" or "Jeshu ben Pandera." Some believe it is likely a mocking name "son of a virgin," a travesty or mix-up of the Greek word *parthenos*, meaning virgin.[12] This was to mock the idea of Jesus' virgin birth and call Him illegitimate, which matches what was said to Jesus in the Gospels (compare John 9:34 and Mark 6:3, where He is called "son of Mary," which in that culture questioned the identity of His father).

Historical reliability

All these references to Jesus were written within 150 years of His life, which is not a long time by the standards of ancient history. For example, Alexander the Great conquered most of the known world and is recognised as a historical figure, not a myth. Yet our best historical source for the details of his life is the work of Plutarch, who lived four centuries after Alexander. Ancient historians value him highly as a reliable source, despite the 400-year gap.

So our non-Christian sources date very early, and our Christian sources even earlier. As E M Blaiklock, formerly Professor of Classics at Auckland University, has written: "My approach to the Classics is historical. And I tell you that the evidence for the life, the death and the resurrection of Christ is better authenticated than most of the facts of ancient history."[13]

2. Major eyewitness sources

Eyewitnesses describe Jesus of Nazareth dying and coming back to life—and these are people who have nothing to gain by telling that story. Of course some would object that all these writers are Christian, and therefore biased. But if they actually witnessed His resurrection, what else would they be but believers?

Let's stop and think about resurrection for a moment. We've all heard of people having heart attacks and being technically dead on the operating table, then being resuscitated. But the Jesus story claims He had been dead from Friday afternoon until Sunday morning and then came back to life.

This is a claim that needs serious investigation. If it's true, it's vitally important. If it's not true, it's fantasy at best or dangerous propaganda at worst.

So let's ask ourselves a few questions:

Are miracles possible? Our tendency is to say no. We like to explain things scientifically, and that's only sensible. We explain the weather by pressure systems, not weather gods. And yet to rule out the possibility of there being a God, and of that God occasionally acting in ways that seem to break natural laws, is a biased approach to the evidence. For the moment, let's not say yes, miracles are possible, and let's not say no. Let's keep an open mind on miracles until we've heard evidence.

And what about these people who claim to have seen Jesus die, then come back to life? Why might they do it? One obvious motive would be money or power. If you write a heart-warming novel about this imaginary Jesus and people like it, then you make money, have fans and are admired and treated well. But the New Testament writers had no such expectations. They were tortured and killed by authorities anxious to suppress the story and its political effects. John bar-Zebedee, writer of an eyewitness biography of Jesus, was ordered by Roman authorities to worship the emperor as Lord. He refused, because Jesus was his Lord, so he was tortured in boiling oil and exiled to a prison island. He was horribly burned, but did not abandon his story, and kept telling it after they let him go. John wrote his biography of Jesus even after seeing his friend and fellow believer Stephen executed by stoning for speaking of Jesus.

These biographers of Jesus wrote even after they had been pursued from place to place, threatened with prison and death, beaten up, and had seen some of their friends killed *for telling this story*. They knew they would not be paid or popular. Their Lord had met a bloody death, so they knew they could be next. And yet they wrote and spoke, travelling to the furthest parts of the world and telling the story to anyone who would listen.

For just one example, the disciple Thomas (sometimes nicknamed Doubting Thomas for his sceptical attitude and initial refusal to believe Jesus could rise from the dead) saw evidence to convince him, and travelled as far as India telling the story of Jesus until someone who wanted to silence him stabbed him to death with a lance.

So these eyewitnesses did not do it for money or power, and kept going in the face of terrifying risk. Why? Could it be that they had really experienced miracles, met God in human form, found it totally life-changing and wanted to tell this truth to everyone else?

Jesus' close friend John wrote about it in this way: "That which was from the beginning, which we have heard, which we have seen with our eyes, which we have looked at and our hands have touched—this

Just the facts

Let's remind ourselves of the basics of the story as the Gospels tell it:

1. Jesus' death and burial

- Jesus was put to death by crucifixion on Friday afternoon.
- A Roman soldier pierced His side with a spear. Blood and water came out (John 19:34).
- The body was wrapped in clean linen cloth (Matthew 27:59).
- The body was placed in a solid rock tomb (Matthew 27:60).
- A large stone was placed in front of the entrance to the tomb (Matthew 27:60).
- A guard (probably Roman) was stationed to secure the tomb (Matthew 27:65).
- A seal was affixed to the stone at the entrance to the tomb (Matthew 27:66).

2. Jesus' resurrection

- Early Sunday morning there was a great earthquake (Matthew 28:1, 2).
- An angel rolled back the stone from the door of the tomb (Matthew 28:2).
- The guards shook with fear and "became like dead men" (Matthew 28:4).
- The angel told the women to tell the other disciples that Jesus was alive and would meet them in Galilee (Matthew 28:7).
- Some of the guards reported the events to the chief priests (Matthew 28:11).
- Soldiers were bribed to say they had fallen asleep and His disciples had stolen His body (Matthew 28:13, 14).
- The soldiers were promised protection if this came to the attention of the governor (Matthew 28:14).

3. Who saw Jesus after His resurrection?[14]

- Sunday morning: Mary Magdalene and "the other Mary" (Matthew 28:1, 9, 10).
- Sunday morning: the other women (Matthew 28:9, 10).
- Sunday afternoon: Cleopas and his friend (Luke 24:13-31).
- Sunday afternoon: Simon Peter (Luke 24:34).
- Sunday evening: Ten apostles (not Thomas or Judas) (John 20:19-24).
- The next Sunday evening: Eleven apostles including Thomas (John 20:26-29).
- Later: Seven by the Lake of Tiberias (John 21).
- Later: More than 500 believers (1 Corinthians 15:6).
- Later: The 11 apostles, who saw Him ascend (Acts 1).
- In vision: Saul/Paul (Acts 9:3-6; 1 Corinthians 15:8).

we proclaim concerning the Word of life. The life appeared; we have seen it and testify to it, and we proclaim to you the eternal life, which was with the Father and has appeared to us. We proclaim to you what we have seen and heard, so that you also may have fellowship with us. And our fellowship is with the Father and with his Son, Jesus Christ. We write this to make your joy complete" (1 John 1:1-4).

See that motivation? He wants us to know that he has seen the Eternal, and is telling us how to find eternal life. He wants us to have friendship with God and with other believers. And he wants to make us happy.

Some strong motivation was needed for these eyewitnesses to spread around the world telling their story, and to start the Christian church, which, within a few centuries, rivalled the power of the Roman Empire itself. But they began by speaking to people who lived right where all these events happened, and inviting them to test their story from what they knew (see, for example, Acts 2).

The Da Vinci Code suggests the early church created Jesus—but if that's true, then who created the early church?

Resurrection questions

As we have said, the resurrection of Jesus is central to Christianity. Anyone wanting to disprove Christianity simply has to disprove the Resurrection. But that has proved a risky task for sceptics. Frank Morison, a British investigator, set out to write a book discrediting the resurrection "myth." After thorough investigation of the evidence, he ended up writing *Who Moved The Stone?* (1958), which is still a classic defence of the truth of Jesus' story. Josh McDowell sat down to poke holes in the Christian belief, but after cross-checking the evidence, he ended up a believer, writing books like *More Than a Carpenter* and *Evidence That Demands a Verdict*. There are many other atheists and critical thinkers who have come to believe in Jesus—among them C S Lewis, of *Narnia* fame, who was shown historical evidence by his friend and fellow Oxford don, J R R Tolkien, author of *The Lord of the Rings*.

Assuming for a moment that the New Testament Gospels are reliable (which we will consider in Chapter 4), anyone wanting to disprove Christianity's central story has the task of explaining each of the following:

- A Roman seal—a sign of Rome's authority—was broken (Matthew 27:66).
- A large stone was moved from the entrance to the tomb while a squad of Roman[15] guards stood watch (Matthew 27:60; 28:2).
- Highly disciplined Roman guards fled their watch and were

bribed by authorities to lie about what happened (Matthew 28:11-15).

▶ The Jerusalem authorities admitted the tomb was empty (Matthew 28:11-15).

▶ The graveclothes, strips of linen that had been wrapped around the body and filled with perfumed spices, were neatly folded in the tomb, not taken or left untidy by hasty grave robbers (John 20:6, 7; cf 19:38-40).

▶ Jesus subsequently appeared to more than 500 witnesses (1 Corinthians 15:6).

▶ Women were described as the first witnesses of the empty tomb (Matthew 28:5-8). If the story was just clever fiction, the writer would not have selected women as the first witnesses because they were legally unable to give evidence in a Jewish court.

▶ The disciples displayed cowardly behaviour at the time of the Crucifixion. Peter denied Jesus three times and the disciples fled the scene of His arrest. But just weeks later, the disciples preached about the empty tomb right there in Jerusalem (Matthew 26:69-75; Mark 14:50; Acts 2:14-32).

▶ It seems the disciples did not expect Jesus to rise and were initially sceptical. But later, they were willing to die for their belief in the Resurrection (Luke 24:10, 11).

▶ The Resurrection message was central to the New Testament and to the preaching of the early Christian church. And the church grew rapidly despite fierce persecution (see, for example, Acts 2:41, 47; 4:33; 5:14; 8:1-4; 23:6-8).

Alternative theories

Alternative theories to the Resurrection attempt to explain what happened to Jesus' body and why the disciples may have believed He rose from the dead.[16] The most common of these are:

▶ **Resuscitation or swoon theory**

This claims Jesus fainted on the cross and woke later.

But Roman soldiers were highly practised with capital punishment, and took special care when executing rebels. A Roman soldier checked Jesus, ready to break His legs so as to speed up death by asphyxiation, but then did not bother because he was sure that He was dead (see John 19:31-33). John, an eyewitness, also saw blood and water—a sign of death—come from the spear-wound on Jesus' side (see John 19:34, 35).

And Jesus had been severely beaten before being crucified. These beatings could easily result in death. Roman soldiers had scourging down to an art form and knew how to stop just short of killing the prisoner, so Jesus was most likely critically injured before He was even crucified. How could someone this weak break out of the linen sheets in which he was tightly wrapped, escape from a rock tomb, and overpower Roman guards (see John 19:38-42)? How could He be alive and well at His many appearances after His resurrection (see John 20:19-29)?

▶ **Conspiracy theory**

This argues that the disciples conspired and deliberately made up a false story.

But none of them "broke" and changed their story under torture and death. What possible motive would they have to die for something they knew was a lie? Also, they were sceptical at first of the story of resurrection, and believed only after seeing the evidence. Their lives were genuinely transformed. They went from depression to faith, giving bold public testimony just days after they were cowering in a locked room.

If this was just a story made up by the disciples, why did the authorities not simply produce Jesus' corpse and disprove the story? They had the power and the motivation to expose a fraud, and Jesus' face could have been easily identified by the thousands of people who had seen Him. Yet the disciples started publicly telling their story right in Jerusalem, where Jesus did much of His work.

▶ **Hallucination theory**

This claims that all the witnesses thought that they saw Jesus, when in fact they just imagined it.

It is possible for a skilled practitioner to hypnotise an individual and even a group for a short time, but Jesus appeared to many different people at different times and places including, on one occasion, 500 eyewitnesses (see 1 Corinthians 15:6).

And hallucination is different from hypnotism. Hallucination is a disorder of sense perception of the external world, often the result of drugs or a psychiatric illness. What are the chances of so many different people at different times experiencing the same false perception?

The disciples touched Him (see Matthew 28:9) and spoke with Him (see Acts 1:3). And it is recorded by an eyewitness and a medically-trained investigator that Jesus ate on at least two occasions after His resurrection (see Luke 24:42, 43; John 21:1-14). Do hallucinations eat, talk and feel physically real?

Again, a story based on hallucination could have been disproved easily if the authorities had produced the body.

A hallucination could not explain the empty tomb.

▶ Theft theory

This one says the disciples stole the dead body of Jesus and made up the story of His resurrection.

Matthew exposes the fact that the Roman guards were bribed to tell this story. The guards went to the religious authorities and reported what really happened. The religious authorities did not want this story getting around, so they told the guards to say that they simply fell asleep on duty and the disciples stole the body (see Matthew 28:11-15).

But this story has three obvious holes. First, how could the guards describe an event that supposedly happened while they were asleep? Second, since Roman soldiers who fell asleep on duty were executed, why were the guards still alive? (The priests assured the guards that they would speak to their commanders so that they would not be executed on the basis of their fabricated story.) And third, how did they sleep through the moving of a large stone right near them?

And what of the disciples? On Friday they were sad, confused, fearing for their lives. Would a clever lie make them suddenly become so bold as to face a detachment of soldiers and steal the body? And why would they fake a resurrection when they did not yet even believe that Jesus would resurrect?

And if someone would knowingly tell a lie for publicity, why would they keep telling it in the face of torture? And how would that fit with the moral and ethical teachings of their faith?

When we examine them more closely, we find these alternative explanations are simply not convincing.

J N D Anderson, former Professor of Oriental Laws at the University of London, concludes, "A number of different theories, each of which might conceivably be applicable to part of the evidence but which do not themselves cohere into an intelligible pattern, can provide no alternative to the one interpretation which fits the whole."[17]

Lord Darling, former Lord Chief Justice of England, said: "The crux of the problem of whether Jesus was, or was not, what He proclaimed Himself to be, must surely depend on the truth or otherwise of the resurrection. On that greatest point we are not merely asked to have faith. In its favour as a living truth there exists such overwhelming evidence, positive and negative, factual and circumstantial that no intelligent jury in the world could fail to bring in a verdict that the resurrection story is true."[18]

In summary: the most likely explanation is that the Resurrection was historically true.

So who or what was Jesus?

So what do we make of Jesus of Nazareth?

Jesus was a great teacher. He gave us classics like "Blessed are the peacemakers" and "Do unto others as you would have them do unto you." One psychiatrist has said that if you took all the best insights of the ages into how to have successful relationships, good mental health and a happy life, and boiled away the excess words, you wouldn't quite equal Jesus Christ's Sermon on the Mount.

The words of Jesus on nonviolence inspired Desmond Tutu, Mohandas Gandhi and Martin Luther King. His words about the poor inspire The Salvation Army, World Vision and countless others. His words have changed people's lives, inspiring generosity and high ideals, bringing out the best and highest in human life. Jesus said, "My words will never pass away." His words have passed into more books, proverbs, artworks, talks, songs, films and internet sites than anyone else's—but they've never passed away. He was a great teacher.

But He also claimed He was God in human form! He said it so many times in so many ways that it cannot be explained away as a later invention.[19] He claimed to be able to give life and take it away. He claimed to be the way to heaven. He claimed He could forgive sins—something only God can do.

So He can't be just a great moral teacher. If someone claims to be God, there are three options:[20]

1. He's mad—there are plenty of people in straitjackets who claim to be God;
2. He's a con man; or
3. He's telling the truth.

So let's have a look at the options.

Option 1: Was Jesus mad? If you read one of His biographies—Matthew, Mark, Luke or John—you see an amazing personality that inspires people. He's even-tempered, whether the crowd is cheering Him or picking up stones to kill Him. He can tolerate hateful attacks, answer questions brilliantly and even predict His own death with emotional balance. It seems highly unlikely He was crazy.

Option 2: Was He a con man? That hardly fits with a great moral teacher. And why would He con? For money? No, He lived simply and gave most of His money to the poor.[21] For power? No, He refused to let people make Him king, and chose to die rather than start a war of rebellion. For popularity? No, He told the truth so much that His enemies outnumbered His friends and eventually killed Him.

So He gained nothing. And if you were clever enough to pull off such a hoax, why would you be stupid enough to do it for no reason?

And could He have faked it anyway? If you wanted to impersonate the Messiah, you'd have to fulfil a number of centuries-old predictions made by Hebrew prophets. First you'd have to be born at the right time, in the right town, from the right tribe—and in a family tracing its ancestry back to King David. Let's say He got lucky with that—but there was also a prediction of the exact date and method of His death. It wouldn't be hard to get your local Roman soldier to kill you—just break the law. But could you choose your date of death? "No, Wednesday doesn't fit my diary. How about Friday?"

And could you choose how you died? "No, no, put that sword away, Captain. It's crucifixion for me, please, and the prediction says I have to be stabbed in the side but no bones must be broken. Owww! I said no bones broken!"

That's ridiculous! Who could fake that? And even if you could, why would you?

So maybe He just got lucky? The mathematician–astronomer Peter Stoner[22] calculated that the chances of fulfilling eight of these prophecies was one in one hundred million million million. That looks like 1 in 100,000,000,000,000,000,000. That's some extraordinary luck. Cover New Zealand with coins a metre deep and ask a blindfolded person to find the one you mark—that's about your chances.

The chances of fulfilling 48 prophecies would be 1 in 10,000,000,000, 000,000,000,000,000,000,000,000,000,000,000,000,000,000,000, 000, 000,000,000,000,000,000,000,000,000,000,000,000,000,000,000, 000,000,000,000,000.

And that's just the beginning. Some scholars estimate Jesus fulfilled 332 prophecies. We could use our smallest type font and you'd need a newspaper full of zeroes.

With evidence like this, can you see why more than a billion people from all cultures believe in Jesus?

Option 3: This one simply makes the most sense. He was telling the truth. He *was* the Truth.

Professor C S Lewis wrote the Narnia series and other great fiction, but he knew the difference between fiction and history. He wrote:

> A man who was merely a man and said the sort of things Jesus said would not be a great moral teacher. He would either be a lunatic—on a level with the man who says he is a poached egg—or else he would be the Devil of Hell. You must make your choice. Either this man was, and is, the Son of God; or else a madman or something worse. You can shut Him up for a fool, you can spit at Him and kill Him as a demon; or you can fall at his feet and call Him Lord and God. But let us not come with any patronising nonsense about His being a great human teacher. He has not left that open to us. He did not intend to.[23]

So those are our options.

Don't worry, this is only the most important decision you will ever make in your life—so no pressure! If this is the first time you have heard the evidence in this way, no-one expects you to decide in five minutes. This is not about trying salesmanship tactics on you. Instead, we are explaining what we wholeheartedly believe to be true, and giving you the chance to decide. Like John, we've found the ring of truth, serious moral challenge, friendship with God and—dare we say—a source of happiness and the meaning of life that we want you to have too. Forever.

As C S Lewis puts it, "I believe in Christianity as I believe that the sun has risen, not only because I see it, but because by it I see everything else."[24]

We will leave the last word to the apostle Peter: "We did not follow cleverly invented stories when we told you about the power and coming of our Lord Jesus Christ, but we were eye-witnesses of his majesty . . . and you will do well to pay attention to it, as to a light shining in a dark place, until the day dawns and the morning star rises in your hearts. Above all, you must understand that no prophecy of Scripture came about by the prophet's own interpretation. For prophecy never had its origin in the will of man, but men spoke from God as they were carried along by the Holy Spirit" (2 Peter 1:16, 19-21).

Chapter 3

NEWTON'S BIG APPLE:
FUTURE PROPHECY

T he Bible is a product of man, my dear. Not of God," says Sir Leigh
Teabing, the eccentric villain of *The Da Vinci Code*. "The Bible did not
fall magically from the clouds. Man created it as a historical record of
tumultuous times, and it evolved through countless translations, additions
and revisions. History has never had a definitive version of the book."[1]

This statement makes major assumptions about the Bible—assumptions
that would be rejected by another English knight who is mentioned in
The Da Vinci Code, Sir Isaac Newton. The novel has Langdon visiting
Newton's tomb looking for clues,[2] and lists Newton as Grand Master of
the Priory of Sion from 1691 to 1727.[3] There is no historical evidence
for this claim, but there is little doubt that Newton was one of the
greatest intellectuals ever, making significant contributions in the fields
of mathematics, optics, planetary gravitation (supposedly after watching
an apple fall), chemistry and of course physics generally (though Einstein
and others have complicated the picture since then). Yet most people
don't know Newton's greatest interest, which is almost ignored in many
biographies.[4] Newton wrote more than a million words about it:[5] prophetic
prediction in the Bible. He was fascinated with the idea of inspired humans
accurately describing the future.

Predictions are easy to get wrong. For example, think of the president
of Decca Records, who rejected the Beatles in 1962, saying, "We don't
like their sound, and guitar music is on the way out anyway." And Darryl

Zanuck, head of 20th Century Fox, who suggested just 60 years ago that "television won't last because people will soon get tired of staring at a plywood box every night." Even Margaret Thatcher said, "It will be years—not in my time—before a woman will become Prime Minister"— just five years before she became British PM in 1979.

We could go on.

Prophetic predictions—the ability to know the future—are fascinating. We're not talking about educated guesses, calculating probability or uttering vague Nostradamus-like predictions that could be interpreted in many different ways. We're talking about accurate knowledge of events it would be humanly impossible to know.

Hard to believe?

Examine one biblical prediction with us. You don't need to believe in the Tooth Fairy—in fact no less a mind than Sir Isaac Newton was convinced by the hard evidence. He investigated ancient historical records, cross-checking one country's dates and events against another's, and against ancient prophecies. His book didn't have a snappy title—*Observations Upon the Prophecies of Daniel and the Apocalypse of St John*—but it was a huge seller in 1733 and is still available online today.[6] After 42 years of study, this great thinker concluded that God had given predictions so that humans could see them come true and believe in God:

> The design of God . . . gave . . . the Prophecies of the Old Testament . . . that after they were fulfilled they might be interpreted by the event, and his own Providence . . . be then manifested thereby to the world. For the event of things predicted many ages before, will then be a convincing argument that the world is governed by providence.[7]

Let's see how he reached that conclusion.

The prophecy Newton discovered

One prophecy particularly caught Newton's attention—and it is relevant to our exploration of Jesus. In this prophecy, a Jewish sage named Daniel predicted key events in the history of Jerusalem and the life and death of Jesus Christ more than 500 years before they happened. And history confirms the accuracy of his vision.

Here is what Daniel wrote: "Know . . . and understand, that from the going forth of the command to restore and build Jerusalem until Messiah the Prince, there shall be seven weeks and sixty-two weeks. . . . And after the sixty-two weeks Messiah shall be cut off, but not for himself; and the people of the prince who is to come shall destroy the city and the sanctuary" (Daniel 9:25, 26. NKJV).

Let's unpack that. The story of Daniel is set in the sixth century BC,[8] when Jerusalem had been ravaged by the armies of Babylon. Daniel, a young nobleman, had been captured in the first siege of Jerusalem in 605 BC and taken to Babylon (modern-day Iraq), where his gifted mind was soon noticed and he was employed in the king's palace. He prayed about his home city of Jerusalem, and received a vision about its future.

1. Jerusalem rebuilt.

The first part of his prediction was that Jerusalem would be rebuilt. This was by no means predictable—many ancient cities never recovered from wartime destruction. The order to rebuild Jerusalem didn't happen until nearly a century after the prediction, after the empire of Babylon had been defeated by the Persians. King Artaxerxes Longimanus decided to let Israel become strong so he could tax them, and use them as a buffer zone against any threat from Egypt. In 457 BC he gave a decree allowing Jews to return home and rebuild[9]—a remarkable action, since many of them were his slaves.

2. Messiah arrives.

This decree to rebuild started a time period of 483 years. This is calculated as "seven weeks" plus "sixty-two weeks," which gives a total of "sixty-nine weeks." *Weeks* here mean weeks of years—seven-year periods very familiar to Judaism. Jewish culture measured time in seven-year periods, just as we naturally think of decades. Their weeks of years had six normal working years then a Sabbath year of recreation and family time. The law of Moses said, "For six years sow your fields . . . but in the seventh year the land is to have a sabbath of rest" (Leviticus 25:3-7). This seven-year period was modelled on the Jewish week, which was six days of work then a Sabbath rest. So when they heard Daniel's prophecy, they would have thought of a "week" of years.[10] As Josh McDowell puts it, "The 7 and 62 weeks are understood as 69 seven-year periods."[11]

$(7x7) + (62x7) = 69x7 = 483$ years

If it took you a while to calculate that, don't feel bad—Newton was better at maths than most of us. So start in the year 457 (when Jerusalem was rebuilt) and count 483 years, and you end up in 27 AD. (If you were out by one, remember there's no year 0.) Interestingly, 27 AD is an accepted date[12] for the start of the public ministry of Jesus Christ, who claimed to be the Messiah or "Anointed One" (see John 4:25, 26).

So far so good.

3. Messiah dies—exactly on time.

The prediction contains more detail: "After the sixty-two weeks, Messiah shall be cut off, but not for himself" (Daniel 9:26, NKJV).

This isn't code. The Hebrew word *Messiah* means a God-given king. "Cut off" means killed violently—an unexpected twist! One would expect God's Messiah king to rule the world, but Daniel foresees that He would appear in Jerusalem and be killed. As we have seen, historians agree that Jesus of Nazareth, called the Christ, was killed on a cross by Roman soldiers after show-trials in Jewish and Roman courts. And the date of 31 AD fits the prediction well.

Even more stunning is the detail that Jesus would die after exactly three-and-a-half years. Daniel wrote, "In the middle of the week he shall bring an end to sacrifice" (Daniel 9:27, NKJV). In the middle of a seven-year "week" is three-and-a-half years—and history confirms that Jesus died after three-and-a-half years of ministry. Jesus' death was the ultimate sacrifice for human guilt and sin.

And it says He's killed "but not for himself." So He died for others. Jesus taught that His death was to pay for the sins of the world. And the expression "cut off" is often used for the death of sacrificial lambs in the Jewish temple;[13] Jesus was called "the Lamb of God who takes away the sin of the world" (John 1:29; and see Isaiah 53:10, another prophet's prediction of the same event).

4. Jerusalem and its Temple destroyed.

But there is still more detail: "And the people of the prince who is to come shall destroy the city and the sanctuary" (Daniel 9:26b, NKJV).

Just a generation after the death of Jesus, the Romans under Titus and Vespasian besieged Jerusalem and attacked it. Titus gave orders that the Temple must not be harmed because it was one of the wonders of the world, but a Roman soldier noticed Jewish soldiers were using the Temple as a hideout, and in a moment of madness, he threw a torch into its roof timbers. It burned to the ground. In the resulting chaos, the Roman army flooded into the city.[14] This happened in the year 70 AD and remains one of the great tragedies of history. (It's why Jewish bridegrooms break a glass under their foot to this day.)

That prediction is inspired—how else do you explain it? A homesick Jew might dream about his city being rebuilt, but how does he foresee his Messiah king arriving five centuries later, dying (a dead Messiah is unthinkable to Jews to this day), then the city being destroyed. How did he predict all that, and with such accurate timing? Too good to be true, or just too good to be human?

But did Daniel cheat?

Some scholars have argued Daniel didn't really make the prediction as long ago as the story claimed—that he cheated and wrote it after all the events happened. If so, he'd be like those annoying people who make sporting predictions on the Monday after the game, not the Friday before. Prophecy after the event isn't really prophecy.

Yet there is too much evidence in Daniel's favour:

1. Among the Dead Sea Scrolls is a manuscript fragment named 4QFlor, which includes Daniel 11:32 and 12:10. These are dated to at least 150 BC.[15] So even if Daniel didn't write in 550 BC, he still wrote his predictions almost 200 years before the events he predicted.

2. Daniel's book appears in the Septuagint (LXX), the Greek translation of the Old Testament. This began in 250 BC and the process continued over a century or more.

3. Daniel is mentioned in the Jewish historical books of Maccabees (written 134-104 BC), which describe the Jewish rebellion against Syrian domination in 175-135 BC. The father of the Maccabees encourages his family to be like the heroes of Jewish history, including Daniel (1 Maccabees 2:59, 60).

4. Alexander the Great read from the book of Daniel in about 330 BC, according to the historian Flavius Josephus. Alexander had just defeated the cities of Tyre and Gaza and marched toward Jerusalem, where some of his advisers wanted him to be ruthlessly violent. But a procession of Jewish priests came out to meet him, so Alexander left his armies behind and went alone with the priests. At the Temple, they showed him Daniel's book, which predicted that the Greeks would defeat the Persians. Alexander was delighted. He did not destroy Jerusalem, and in fact he gave them a tax-free year every seventh year so they could enjoy their "Sabbath year."[16] This dates Daniel's book to well before 330 BC.

There is more evidence to suggest Daniel knew Babylon first-hand,[17] but this is enough to demonstrate that he did not cheat. He wrote his predictions centuries before the events he predicted.

Is it just how you read it?

You could ask whether Daniel wrote dozens or hundreds of predictions that failed, and we've chosen only to tell you about those that worked. The simple answer is no. But check out his book for yourself.

And neither is it just a matter of interpretation. When you reread the wording, it's exact: it spells out the city, mentions a starting date confirmed by history, gives a real time period, and describes the death of the Messiah and, soon after, the destruction of Jerusalem and its Temple. There's no symbolism or mumbo jumbo. Some things take a bit of explaining 25 centuries later in a different culture, but it's clear, literal language.[18]

How does that help us?

We began this chapter with Langdon's comment that the Bible is merely human. But Sir Isaac Newton and Daniel throw that into serious doubt.

Doesn't Daniel's humanly impossible prediction give evidence to believe in a personal God, who is intelligent enough to know the future? (That is great news for anyone who doesn't like what they see or hear on the news.)

Doesn't it suggest that this God is not distant and uninvolved, but caring enough to offer this type of guidance to the human race? (That is great news for anyone who feels like their life could use some guidance and protection.)

And doesn't this God seem involved with Jesus Christ, suggesting His life and death are important events to the human race?

This all deserves serious consideration.

Sir Isaac Newton thought so. After years of study, he called this prediction "the foundation stone of the Christian religion."[19] Like all foundations, it is heavy and requires a lot of digging—but isn't it great to know that faith and hope are built on something solid?

·

Chapter 4

THE DA VINCI CODE
AND THE BIBLE

*T*he *Da Vinci Code* claims Christianity is built on a cover-up, and so it questions the credibility of the Bible. We have already noticed Leigh Teabing's statement to Sophie:

> The Bible is a product of *man*, my dear. Not of God. The Bible did not fall magically from the clouds. Man created it as a historical record of tumultuous times, and it evolved through countless translations, additions and revisions. History has never had a definitive version of the book.[1]

He continues:

> More than 80 gospels were considered for the New Testament, and yet only a relative few were chosen for inclusion—Matthew, Mark, Luke and John among them.[2]

> The Bible, as we know it today, was collated by the pagan Roman emperor Constantine the Great.[3] . . . Constantine commissioned and financed a new Bible, which omitted those gospels that spoke of Christ's human traits and embellished those gospels that made Him godlike. The earlier gospels were outlawed, gathered up, and burned.[4]

And this conversation also includes a further couple of statements we have already looked at:

> Fortunately for historians . . . some of the gospels that
> Constantine attempted to eradicate managed to survive. The
> Dead Sea Scrolls were found in the 1950s hidden in a cave near
> Qumran in the Judaean desert. And, of course, the Coptic
> Scrolls in 1945 at Nag Hammadi.[5]

Teabing returns to these topics a little later: ". . . the Nag Hammadi
and Dead Sea Scrolls . . . the earliest Christian records. Troublingly they
do not match up with the gospels in the Bible."[6]

So let's consider these claims.

The Dead Sea Scrolls

As we have seen, the statements regarding the Dead Sea Scrolls reveal
some embarrassingly huge mistakes in Brown's research. The Dead Sea
Scrolls are Jewish books—nothing to do with the early Christians and
written at least a century before Christ. This can be verified by any good
encyclopedia.

But even more embarrassingly for Brown's case, these Dead Sea Scrolls
actually confirm the accurate transmission of a large part of the Bible.
The Christian Bible is made up of the Old Testament, a collection of
Jewish books written between approximately 1500 BC and 430 BC, and
the New Testament, a collection of documents about the life of Jesus and
the early church, written between 10 and 60 years after Jesus lived.[7]

Brown seems to confuse the Old and New Testaments, but they are
significantly different. The Old Testament was written mainly in Hebrew,
the Jewish language, while the New Testament was written in Greek,
the language of the empire conquered by Alexander the Great's troops.
Scholars estimate the Old Testament was recognised as a collection by
around 250 BC. At around that time scholars began translating it into
Greek, producing the Septuagint, of which we have copies today.

For a long time scholars had no manuscript copies of the Old Testament
in its original Hebrew language before about 1000 AD, and critics claimed
that mistakes and changes had crept into the Old Testament. But in
the mid-20th century, Arab shepherds accidentally discovered ancient
documents stored in 11 caves near Qumran in Israel. Dry conditions had
preserved the manuscripts pretty well. Scholars called it the find of the
century, and some have devoted their entire careers to studying these

manuscripts. The most important upshot is that we can compare the manuscripts of around 1000 AD with these manuscripts from before the time of Christ. Brown might be interested to know that while there are some human scribal errors—a letter here, a word there—there is more than 99 per cent[8] agreement between what is in the Bible today and what was found in these completely independent manuscripts from 2000 years ago. So much for "additions and revisions."

Perhaps Brown shouldn't have mentioned the Dead Sea Scrolls, because they are facts that do stand in the way of his good story. They support the accuracy of a large part of the Bible.

The Nag Hammadi manuscripts

These were the Gnostic "gospels" we have previously discussed. They were written much later than the accepted Gospels by writers with a Gnostic—not Christian—view of Jesus. The Roman Catholic and other churches have not tried to suppress these Gnostic writings since their discovery. Rather, Christian scholars have welcomed them as fascinating insights into the Gnostic religion, which is important background to the history of early Christianity. And, as we have already discovered, they are not as pro-women as Brown imagines, or as pro-women as Jesus Himself.

In short, these Gnostic "gospels" were never seriously considered as gospels to be included in the Bible.

Changing the Bible?

Let's say someone like the Roman emperor wanted to make some "additions and revisions" to the existing Bible in the fourth century, more than 300 years after the New Testament was written. If just one official copy of the Bible were etched in silver in a library somewhere, the task would be simple: change the original, destroy any old copies, kill anyone who objected and perhaps keep the secret. But there is a problem with such a hypothetical scenario. By the fourth century, copies were scattered all over the world.

How this happened is a story in itself. For example, John writes Jesus' biography and it is read in the churches in Turkey where John worked. The original version is written in Greek on papyrus, a writing material made from reeds. It circulates from church to church and is so well received that someone decides to make a copy of it.

With the printing press still 1400 years in the future, specially trained scribes copied it by hand. This took weeks—and was expensive. The average working person could never hope to own even one scroll in their lifetime, and may not have been able to read anyway. The local church may have owned a complete set of the Bible scrolls and read from them publicly. These copies spread quickly to churches across the then-known world, and were recopied in various countries. By the time of Constantine, thousands of copies could be found in far-flung places around the world, and he could never hope to change them all.

And, significantly, the original New Testament documents were lost, meaning there is no original Gospel of John in a library somewhere for a Constantine to change. But there are copies preserved from the many countries to which Christianity spread, especially those with hot, dry climates where manuscripts last longer.

Were all these manuscripts identical? Frankly, no—and that makes sense. Totally identical copies in so many places would be a little too good to be true. Small human errors crept in during the copying process. And if one copyist made a mistake in their manuscript, all those who copied from that manuscript would have the same mistake.

So does this mean today's Bible is hopelessly inaccurate? Not at all. The modern science of textual criticism is devoted to piecing together all the "manuscript families" in an attempt to work out what the original text said. And on the whole, these differences are tiny, so that no major doctrine or belief of Christianity is affected. Modern Bible translations like the New International Version are quite honest about the small differences between manuscripts. They list them in footnotes so any reader who cares about these things is fully informed.

Textual criticism is a huge topic and you can do doctorates in it at university, but the bottom line for our purposes is this:

- most of the changes in the New Testament are a letter here, a word there—this is not a secret; Bible translations are open about it, and
- the science of textual criticism can put it all together with a high degree of accuracy.

No manuscripts show evidence of serious rewriting or tampering by a later hand. This is very strong evidence that the Bible we have today is functionally identical to the original version.

Textual variations in the Gospel of Mark

We can find a number of textual variations in the Gospel of Mark, which are identified in the footnotes in the New International Version (NIV) and other translations. Let's consider a few examples to see how much difference they might make to our understanding of Jesus and the stories of His life.

We have a textual difference in the very first verse:

Mark 1:1: "The beginning of the gospel about Jesus Christ, the Son of God."

The NIV footnote reads, "Some manuscripts do not have *the Son of God.*" So some manuscripts just have, "The beginning of the gospel of Jesus Christ," and don't include the words *the Son of God.*

We can guess that one scribe added those words to the text, or maybe another scribe left them out. We are not sure if they were in the original or not. But does this cast doubt over whether Jesus really was the Son of God? No. Even if those words were not in the original, we only have to read nine verses further and we find a voice from heaven saying to Jesus, "You are my Son, whom I love; with you I am well pleased" (Mark 1:11). And that story is in all the manuscripts. So even if Mark 1:1 doesn't have the words *the Son of God,* the idea is clear later in the chapter.

Then there's not another textual variant listed until chapter 3:

Mark 3:14: "He appointed twelve—designating them apostles—that they might be with him and that he might send them out to preach."

And the NIV footnote says, "Some manuscripts do not have *designating them apostles.*" So either one scribe accidentally left that out—or another added it in. But we can find other places in the New Testament where Christ's 12 disciples are called apostles, such as a few chapters later in Mark 6:30, plus six occurrences in Luke. The fact remains whether these words are left in or out.

Three more quick ones:

Mark 7:4 says of the Jewish religious leaders, "When they come from the market-place they do not eat unless they wash. And they observe many other traditions, such as the washing of cups, pitchers and kettles."

And the footnote tells us that some manuscripts leave out the word *cups* and make the list read "pitchers, kettles and dining couches." Is this a significant change?

A few verses later, Mark records Jesus offering some honest criticism to some religious leaders. Mark 7:9: "And he said to them: 'You have a fine way of setting aside the commands of God in order to observe your own traditions!'"

The footnote tells us some manuscripts don't say "observe your traditions," but actually say "set up your traditions." That's not exactly a serious difference.

Then one story begins with this line (Mark 7:24): "Jesus left that place and went to the vicinity of Tyre."

And the footnote says some manuscripts read "Tyre and Sidon." Tyre and Sidon were neighbouring cities, so it hardly matters whether you say you're in the area of one or both. It means the same thing.

The last chapter of Mark also gives us the chance to examine the largest textual difference in the New Testament. Two early Greek manuscripts do not include the last 12 verses. Some scholars believe the last part was torn off, and that other versions were added later by well-intentioned copyists because the book ended abruptly. Yet other scholars argue that the last 12 verses are authentic because they are in the vast majority of early manscripts, and are quoted in Christian writers as early as the second century.

Without going into all the arguments either way, how do we deal with this? If there is any question about the authenticity of a verse, it should be used carefully: no major historical claim or belief should be based on it alone. But then major beliefs should usually be cross-checked by more than one text to make sure we are not making a mistake in interpretation. So this is no major problem. Also, a questioned passage should be cross-checked with other Gospels. Mark 16:9-11 is similar to Luke 24:10, 11; verses 12-14 seem like a shorter version of the story in Luke 24:13-15; verse 15 is similar to Matthew 28:18-20. Verse 19 compares to Luke 24:51. Verses 17, 18 contain some unique material (for example, Jesus' mention of tongues and being poison-proof) but they are comparable to His other comments on signs.

These questions need not unsettle confidence in the New Testament. At worst, there are 12 disputed verses, which are largely backed up in other material anyway. Compared to the large-scale "additions and revisions" claimed by Brown, this is very small.

Testing sources

When ancient historians want to assess the accuracy of a copy of an ancient document, they ask two major questions:

1. How many copies do we have?

More than 24,970 New Testament manuscripts are in existence, of which 5686 are Greek manuscripts.[9] Other ancient documents have far fewer copies still around. The best-attested is Homer's *Iliad*, with 643 copies. Most well-respected ancient literature has only a handful of manuscripts.[10]

2. How much time separates the available copies from the originals?

In the Bible's case, not long.[11]

▶ The University of Manchester has a manuscript that experts agree dates between 115 and 130 AD. It contains several verses from the Gospel of John. It's named P52, or the John Rylands Manuscript after the wealthy textile manufacturer who helped finance the discovery.

▶ In Geneva, Switzerland, is a papyrus dated to 150-200 AD. It contains all of John's Gospel except for some gaps due to damage, and is called the Bodmer Papyrus II.

▶ A manuscript dated to 200 AD is in a museum in Dublin, Ireland, and contains large parts of the New Testament. It's named P45, or the Chester Beatty papyrus after Sir Alfred Chester Beatty, a copper-mining millionaire who helped fund the research.

So if the Gospels were written in the 50s-60s AD, our oldest manuscripts are only about 60 years removed. And as backup, we have many quotations from the Gospels—and other New Testament books—recorded in the writings of Apostolic Fathers like Clement and Ignatius around 100 AD, the earliest Christian writings after the New Testament.

On both those questions, the Gospels stack up much better than any other ancient document, bar none. We're not saying that this proves their content is true, but it does make Brown's claim about "countless . . . additions and revisions" look like a great line for a novel, but not reliable history.

When was the New Testament written?

There has been a lot of debate about this, but the crucifixion of Jesus Christ—generally accepted as occurring approximately 31 AD—provides a reference point. Independent, non-Christian authors such as Tacitus and Josephus confirm that He was crucified in Judea sometime between 26 and 36 AD.[12]

Internal evidence also provides a clue as to the dating of the New Testament documents. For example, the book of Acts does not record the death of the apostle Paul, who was martyred by Emperor Nero around 67-68 AD, a fact that suggests Acts was written earlier.[13] Luke was written earlier than that by the same author, and scholars believe the Gospel of Mark was written even closer to the events it describes. Another clue is found in 1 Corinthians 15, where the apostle Paul refers to 500 people who were witnesses of the resurrection of Jesus, many of whom were still alive at the time he wrote the book.

Researcher Darrell Bock dates the writings of Paul between 50 and 68 AD,[14] while Paul Barnett suggests the range 50-65 AD, and puts the Gospels of Matthew, Mark and Luke "sometime between the sixties and eighties." Barnett adds, "These dates are debated among scholars, and I use the most conservative range."[15]

So did Constantine change the Bible?

Constantine was emperor of the Roman Empire from 313 to 337 AD. He favoured Christianity, perhaps for political reasons, and it is debatable how much he himself became a Christian because he participated in various pagan practices throughout his life.

Constantine did finance the production of a Bible, although he did not compile it or edit it. There is no evidence he omitted some Gospels and embellished others, and good evidence that he did not, for the following reasons:

1. As we have seen, the Gospels were too widely spread around the world for him to access most of the copies.

2. We have copies of Gospel manuscripts from 200 years before Constantine, and they match Gospel manuscripts from after his time.

3. As backup, we have parts of these Gospels quoted in the writings of early church leaders well before 325, when Brown claims they were changed at the church Council of Nicaea.

4. We have records of Constantine ordering the burning of certain writings, like those of the heretic Arius, but no mention of him burning Gospels of any kind—Christian or Gnostic. It wasn't Constantine who excluded the Gnostic "gospels." The early church had already rejected them.

Why were certain books included and others excluded?

Many books circulated in the early church. Examples include "The Epistle of Barnabas," "The Shepherd of Hermas" as well as the first and second letters of Clement. Why were they left out of the New Testament?

The early church had to be very clear about which writings were genuine and "inspired" by God. Remember they were being persecuted and killed for their faith, and no-one would want to die for a lie or a fake document. So they examined the writings carefully, using three main tests:

1. Known authorship by an apostle or an associate of an apostle;
2. Content agreeing with the received apostolic teaching in the church; and
3. Widespread acceptance within the Christian church community.

It seems there were frauds around from the earliest times. Paul began signing all his own letters because of impostors (2 Thessalonians 3:17; 2:2).

Why would someone write a false letter?

▶ To express their point of view. For example, to argue for Gnosticism.

▶ To speculate about Jesus' childhood or some other information we are not given.

▶ Simply to tell exciting stories.

▶ Even, as Christianity became less dangerous and more popular, to make money.

▶ Sincere intentions. One Asian church official wrote *The Acts of Paul*—100 years after Paul died! His excuse was that he did it "for the love of Paul." But he was defrocked.[16] Sincerity is not to be confused with truth or divine inspiration.

So the early church carefully tested would-be "scriptures." Yet they regarded the genuine Scriptures as having more authority than the church itself. The church did not create that authority, but merely recognised it. F F Bruce states, "One thing must be emphatically stated. The New Testament books did not become authoritative for the Church because they were formally included in a canonical list; on the contrary, the Church included them in her canon because she already regarded them as divinely inspired, recognising their innate worth and generally apostolic authority, direct and indirect."[17]

When was the collection completed?

The four Gospels were brought together soon after the writing of the Gospel of John.[18] The fourfold collection was actually known as "The Gospel" early in the second century. In about 170 AD, Tatian produced a harmony of the Gospels: this was a continuous narrative incorporating the four Gospels. By 180—as noted in the writings of Irenaeus, Bishop of Lyons—the four Gospels had an established and authoritative position in the church.

The book of Acts was accepted early, as it was written by Luke, the author of the third Gospel, and shared the authority and prestige of that work.

The writings of Paul were also accepted early. Ignatius (around 115) seems to be acquainted with collections of Paul's writings. And even a biblical passage (2 Peter 3:15, 16) makes mention of at least some of Paul's writings as being authoritative in the church.

Origen (185-254) states that the following writings were accepted by all: the four Gospels, Acts, 13 Pauline writings, 1 Peter, 1 John and Revelation. Writings still disputed by some included Hebrews, 2 Peter, 2 and 3 John, James and Jude.[19]

Eusebius (c 260-c 340) mentions that all of the current New Testament books were widely accepted except James, Jude, 2 Peter, 2 and 3 John. These were accepted by the majority, but nevertheless disputed by some.[20]

In 367, Athanasius records the first list of canonical books comprising the 27 books of the current New Testament. The Councils of Hippo (393) and Carthage (397) were the first to make a formal list of the 27 accepted books of the New Testament, though they simply recognised an existing collection widely acknowledged before that. This list is still accepted today.

Christians believe God managed the process of forming the Bible. This makes sense if one accepts the idea of a personal God who has the ability to work in human history to shape a trustworthy Bible.

What happened at the Council of Nicaea?

Brown says Constantine "upgraded Jesus' status almost four centuries after Jesus' death." Brown's character Teabing claims the Council of Nicaea (325) officially voted that Jesus should be upgraded to "the Son of God," and it was "a relatively close vote at that."

There was a church Council in Nicaea in 325 under the patronage of the Roman emperor Constantine. But the Council did not debate whether or not Jesus was divine. It debated whether He had always existed as God, or had been created by God the Father. A popular teacher named Arius had been teaching that Jesus had been created by God. This was a strange idea to Christianity, so church leaders from most of the known world got together to deal with it.

Saying Jesus was the first creation actually made Him subordinate to God the Father. Bishops like Athanasius argued that Christ had always existed, and that He was fully divine. He was of the same essence and substance as the Father. This had been long understood as orthodox Christian teaching, and the church maintained that position.

Nobody was arguing Jesus was merely human, as *The Da Vinci Code* claims. Christians for almost 300 years had agreed He was divine.[21]

And the vote at Nicaea? It never happened. The bishops—numbering between 200 and 318 at various times in the conference[22]—discussed Arius' teaching versus accepted Christian teaching. Only five bishops objected at any time to some of the wording of the creed, and only two refused to sign. Their names were Theonas and Secundus, and they refused to sign, possibly for political reasons—the creed contained a clause that would have brought them under the control of a bishop in Alexandria.[23]

Eventually the council issued a statement that expressed traditional Christian doctrine that God the Father and Jesus Christ His Son are "of one being" and "of one substance." They said Jesus Christ was "begotten, not made," and was "God from God, Light from Light, true God from true God." The views of Arius were condemned.[24]

So Brown was wrong to say it was a "close vote": there was no vote and, even if there had been, 198 to 2 would not be a close vote.

Has the Bible been changed in translation?

Some critics say the Bible's translation has been biased to say what the church wants. But it's not just Christians who translate it. Universities have independent specialists from many cultures and religions, and some of no religion, who study ancient languages. Each language has its own objective rules and meanings in the public domain. All translations are open to scrutiny. If you take almost any published New Testament translation to a professor of classics, he or she will say it is a fair and objective translation of the Greek.[25]

Of course, variations occur between translations. Some are word-for-word—"formal equivalence translations"—that translate what the original text literally says and let the reader work out the meaning. These tend to be precise but can be difficult to read. Other translations are more thought-for-thought —"dynamic equivalence translations"—tending to explain and perhaps simplify the text. These are often easier reading.

However, on the whole, the various versions of the Bible use different words but express very much the same ideas.

A reliable book

So there are solid reasons to believe the Bible is accurate. We can be confident that the New Testament is historically reliable and has remained functionally identical for almost 2000 years.

Chapter 5

SEX AND SEXISM

*T*he *Da Vinci Code* is a sexy book. But what kind of sex? The book depicts two major attitudes, each connected with a major way of viewing the world. But it leaves out a third alternative.

1. "Thou shalt not . . ."

The first view of sex is the "Thou shalt not . . ." approach of the church as Brown sees it. His character Leigh Teabing describes church leaders who rigidly control other people's sex lives, while numbers of them abuse children and cover up for colleagues who do so.

The message is that Chrisianity is not sexy, and its teachings on sex are so hopelessly extreme that even its leaders can't follow them.

And the church seems to prefer bodily pain for the supposed good of the soul rather than pleasure. For the monk Silas, "pain is good."[1] He wears a *cilice* or barbed strap around his thigh and whips himself bloody in "corporal mortification"[2] (which is from Latin words meaning literally "to put the body to death").

Is this real Christianity?

Let's admit that the church has a horrendous record on sexual crimes. Extreme rules such as enforced celibacy—not a biblical command—may produce imbalance in other directions. These extreme ideas on sex, which have made life so difficult for well-intentioned followers and wrecked the lives of so many victims, have no place in the teaching of Jesus of Nazareth, who taught a healthy attitude to sex. Without going heavily into historical theology, we can observe that the balanced teaching of

Jesus was gradually replaced in the church by other ideas.

Perhaps the most extreme example of this was the Christian thinker Augustine (354-450). Augustine was born into Christianity, but during his early adulthood he was sexually promiscuous and almost abandoned his spirituality. He had a child with a mistress and started to realise that sex was not just a game. Eventually he began looking for God again and trying to revive his faith, but was extremely guilty about his previous behaviour and memories, and still felt serious sexual temptation.

Eventually he went to the extreme of cutting off his own testicles in an attempt to avoid sexual temptation. Even that didn't work; he was still tortured by sexual fantasy. He sent his mistress away—as though she was the problem—and also banished his child in a bizarre attempt to move past his guilt. And he went on to spend his life in thought and scholarship. His major project was to make Christian thinking fit with the fashionable neo-Platonic philosophy inherited from the Greek thinker Plato.

One thing Augustine borrowed was Plato's idea that the body was corrupt and sinful, while the soul and mind were the spark of God and the source of good. (The Gnostics taught something similar, as you'll remember from a previous chapter.) This is not a biblical idea, because the Bible teaches God created the human body and called it "very good." And Augustine's own experience should have shown him it was unrealistic. Even when he removed his testicles, he was still mentally tempted, which should have shown him that his sin problem was not only in his body but in his mind and spirit.

But he borrowed Plato's idea of the Platonic relationship, not involving the body but only the mind and spirit. Augustine taught that was the ideal relationship for Christians: no sex, just spiritual closeness. This was straight from Plato, not from Christ, and yet the church accepted it. Augustine was incredibly influential on the church for hundreds of years. His thinking became official church doctrine.

No wonder the medieval church had some extreme ideas about sex.

2. Free love for nature worshippers

The novel advocates a second attitude to sex. We might call this free love for nature worshippers. Sophie remembers as a university student stumbling in on an orgy at her grandfather's home, and witnessing him having sex with a woman in the middle of a chanting circle of masked people.[3] She was shocked and hurt, and broke off contact with him. Now Langdon explains that this was a secret society performing a ritual called *Hieros Gamos*. He tells Sophie about it:

> He explained that although what she saw probably looked like a sex ritual, Hieros Gamos had nothing to do with eroticism. It was a spiritual act. Historically, intercourse was the act through which male and female experienced God. The ancients believed that the male was spiritually incomplete until he had carnal knowledge of the sacred feminine. Physical union with the female remained the sole means through which man could become spiritually complete and ultimately achieve *gnosis*—knowledge of the divine. Since the days of Isis, sex rites had been considered man's only bridge from earth to heaven. "By communing with women," Landgon said, "man could achieve a climactic instant when his mind went totally blank and he could see God."
>
> Sophie looked sceptical. "Orgasm as prayer?"[4]

This statement invites a number of questions:

1. Does it make sense to say that a sex rite has "nothing to do with eroticism"?
2. Who does Brown mean by "the ancients"? Which society? When in history? Has any mainstream religion ever taught that sex was "man's only bridge . . . to heaven"? What about prayer, meditation or prophecy?
3. This is about how men achieve union with the divine. What about women? Why aren't they mentioned in a book promoting equality?
4. How does a blank mind help one understand or feel God anyway? Isn't the mind, in all its varied ability to appreciate emotion, beauty, logic and the like, our only way to connect with God?

But Langdon's lecture continues:

> "Sophie," Langdon said quietly, "it's important to remember that the ancients' view of sex was entirely opposite from ours today. Sex begot new life—the ultimate miracle—and miracles

could be performed only by a god. The ability of the woman to produce new life from her womb made her sacred. A god. Intercourse was the revered union of the two halves of the human spirit—male and female—through which the male could find spiritual wholeness and communion with God. What you saw was not about sex, it was about spirituality."

He gave her a moment. Admittedly, the concept of sex as a pathway to God was mind-boggling at first.[5]

But this raises further questions:

5. Has anyone ever really taught that only women produce life?

6. Why is the highly intelligent Sophie being lectured so much by two older males?

And if you believed all of this, how would you run your sex life? Here is Langdon's advice to his students:

"The next time you find yourself with a woman, look in your heart and see if you cannot approach sex as a mystical, spiritual act. Challenge yourself to find that spark of divinity that man can only achieve through union with the sacred feminine."

The women all smiled knowingly, nodding.

The men exchanged dubious giggles and off-colour jokes.

Langdon sighed. College men were still boys.[6]

That may sound very perceptive and spiritual if you read it quickly, but stop and think about it. "Next time you're with a woman . . ." Which woman? Any woman? The one you love and respect? And how would you know that spark of divinity if you woke up in bed with it? What if "free love" was against good spiritual practice? What if spirituality was really all about focused love and commitment and self-control? What if intimacy worked best with only one person?

And all this advice is to men. Where is advice for women? How do they find the spark of divinity? Why does the supposed feminist Langdon not mention this important point? Or does he think "all" the women already know? Does this mean they are spiritually superior to men? How would that make sense if Langdon says male and female are both parts of divine spirit? And are all women really enlightened about sex and God? Even those who have had painful sexual experiences? Even agnostics and atheists who do not believe in the spiritual? It just doesn't make sense.

Brown also writes about sex in biblical history: "Langdon's Jewish students always looked flabbergasted when he told them that early Jewish tradition involved ritualistic sex. *In the Temple, no less.* . . . Men seeking spiritual wholeness came to the Temple to visit priestesses—or *hierodules*—with whom they made love and experienced the divine through physical union. The Jewish tetragrammaton YHWH—the sacred name of God—in fact derived from Jehovah, an androgynous physical union between the masculine *Jah* and the pre-Hebraic name for Eve, *Havah*."[7]

In this instance, he's half-right. There were many times in Jewish history, as recorded in the Old Testament or Hebrew Bible, when sex was used in worship, including sacred prostitution in the Temple. This was also standard practice for centuries in many of the nations around Israel. But Brown leaves out an important point: sexualised worship happened when Judaism became corrupted by copying other nations, and the Bible writers and prophets were always against it. And Israel always suffered for it.

Moses made a clear prohibition from the earliest times: "No Israelite man or woman is to become a shrine-prostitute" (Deuteronomy 23:17). Yet sexualised worship was a problem for Israel from the first, when the Jewish slaves were escaping Egypt. After they have an orgiastic party trying to worship calf gods and Yahweh at the same time, Moses appears and reminds them of the Ten Commandments (Exodus 32). Only months later, a similar worship orgy happens (see Numbers 25:1-3). An invitation from a curvy neighbour to a sexual–spiritual celebration of her gods was almost irresistible to the men of Israel, and it had a damaging spiritual and moral effect.

These "fertility religions" of Israel's neighbours were so popular because they promised to make you rich through good crops, and also made worship very sexy—it was great marketing. It seems that on every second page of the Old Testament, the people of Israel were "prostituting" themselves in this way (see, for example, 1 Kings 14:24 and Job 36:14). Various kings led revivals of true religion and tried to clean up these unlawful practices (see 2 Kings 23:7), but Israel seemed addicted. One of the last prophets gave the disgusting image of a father and son both sleeping with the same shrine prostitute, and lying down drunk beside a pagan altar, spending money they had taken from the poor (see Amos

2:7, 8). This was religion at its very worst: abusing women, destroying family values and relationships, and spreading disease.

Brown is right about this history, but he infers this was the original Jewish way of worshipping in the Temple. That's plain wrong.

The original Judaism was all about monotheism and monogamy—one God, one marriage partner. The people often conveniently forgot that, but it remained the true Judaism.

And as far as Brown's theory about God's name including a goddess: YHWH is the personal name of God revealed to Moses, but originally written in Hebrew without vowels. It most likely comes from the verb "to be" and means something like "I AM" or "I WILL BE WHAT I WILL BE." *Jehovah* or *Yahweh* are scholars' best guesses as to how it was pronounced, but we are not sure. And Eve's name is not *Havah,* it's *Chava* (with a different initial letter in Hebrew). Basic spelling shows us that *Chavah* has never been part of Yahweh. Eve's name *Chavah* comes from the word *chayah,* which means life,[8] and Eve is called the mother of all living.

Again, Brown's report card reads A+ for Creative Writing but F for History and Hebrew language. And we need to look elsewhere to find Judaism's attitude to sex and spirituality. It doesn't get a mention in *The Da Vinci Code.*

3. Biblical view of sex

Judaism viewed sex as God's gift for our enjoyment within the love and commitment of a marriage. And Jesus, being a Jew, had this biblical view.

From the beginning, God created Adam and Eve "naked . . . and . . . not ashamed," designing the human spirit and body for enjoyment of sex and all His good gifts. God looks at this creation and calls it "very good" (Genesis 2:25; 1:31, NKJV). Importantly, God makes both male and female in His own image (see Genesis 1:27, 28). Both male and female bear the image of God. And this includes their sexuality, because God tells them to "be fruitful and multiply," and He's not talking about mathematics. Sex is part of God's blessing, and results in fruitfulness and creation/procreation.

And there are passages in the Bible that celebrate the God-given joy of sex. For example, Proverbs 5:18-20: "May you rejoice in the wife of your youth. A loving doe, a graceful deer—may her breasts satisfy you always, may you ever be captivated by her love. Why be captivated, my son, by an adulteress?"

There is a whole collection of erotic poetry in the Bible, known as the Song of Solomon (or Song of Songs). It describes in sensual detail the love of a woman and a man. In it, the woman speaks at least as much as the man, and is his equal in every way—even though he is a king.

Some people are shocked to find that in the Bible. But it is there. What could it be trying to tell us?

1. That God wants humans to enjoy love and sex. God is not a killjoy.

2. That sex and companionship are ideal in a marriage. The woman says of her husband, "This is my lover, this is my friend" (Song of Songs 5:16).

3. That the Bible—unlike body-crushing Gnostic asceticism and legalistic religions—does not see sex as something to be "suppressed, denied and imprisoned." Ascetic religion "fears that if the joy of physical love is not condemned," the mind will "forget spiritual things" and "plunge into ever deeper corruption." This actually underestimates God's ability to bring healing to the human heart and focus us on positive things. Legal religion tries to build a protective wall around the human heart, but only ends up separating the person further from God and giving them a false hope of being able to be good by their own efforts. Real biblical religion goes to the heart. It believes God's creation of the body was a good thing, and that God can teach believers how to live well.[9]

4. The church needs to hear this! Remember Augustine, who quoted Plato's ideas about the bad body? Many Christians are still making that mistake. As Christian scholar Gollwitzer has written, "No one church has done better than another; all have operated under the prejudice of a Neoplatonic hostility to the body and to sex."[10]

5. Sex is meant to bring a loving couple closer in love. It's not just to share with anyone, but is about building intimacy. Theologians call this the "unitive" aspect of sex,[11] making man and woman into "one flesh"—and it's more important than mere reproduction. Some churches still teach that sex is moral only if it is engaged in for reproduction, but the Bible does not say that.[12]

6. A human being is not a good soul in a bad body. As Tremper Longman III puts it, "God is interested in us as whole people. We are not souls encased in a husk of flesh. The Song [of Solomon] celebrates the joys of physical touch, the exhilaration of exotic scents, the sweet sound of an intimate voice, the taste of another's body. Furthermore, the book explores human emotion—the thrill and power of love as well as its often attendant pain. The Song affirms human love, intimate relationship, sensuality and sexuality."[13]

7. The Song of Solomon is very different from the love poems we've found from the fertility religions of Mesopotamia, Canaanite and Egyptian cults. It does not mention love play among the gods, and never suggests that the couple's sexuality will help the gods get busy renewing nature.[14] Methodist scholar John Snaith calls it "a non-mythological, non-cultic, non-idolatrous, outright, open celebration of God-given sexual love."[15]

8. That sex and spirituality are different. Baptist theologian Duane Garrett says, "Simply put, the act of sex is not a religious act. This may seem obvious enough to some, but ancient pagans would have by no means shared this view. The cults of the ancient world, from India to the Mediterranean, promoted sexuality as a ritual of religious devotion. . . . In the modern era some recent theological perspectives (particularly radical feminist theology) have sought once again to merge religion and eroticism in a manner unknown in the West since pre-Christian paganism."[16]

Jesus and sex

We must remember Jesus was a Jew, and inherited all the Old Testament literature with its healthy attitudes to sex. When people asked him about the rights and wrongs of sex, he quoted Genesis, showing Adam and Eve as God's ideal (see Matthew 19:4-8). He obviously knew the Song of Solomon (see Matthew 6:28; Revelation 3:20 also alludes to Song of Songs 5:2-5).

Jesus encouraged marriage—one of His priorities after beginning His public work was to attend a wedding where He performed His first miracle (see John 2:1-11).

What about celibacy? "Jesus had a mission," writes Margaret George, author of *Mary, Called Magdalene*. "I cannot believe He would take on a wife and family knowing what would happen to Him, just in human terms."[17] Certainly Christ knew He would die young (see Matthew 16:21) and so presumably He decided it would be irresponsible to marry. Second, if Christ had left descendants, they might claim special status—like the Merovingians in Brown's novel—when Jesus was more interested in equality (see Luke 11:27, 28).

Jesus taught that marriage is God's ideal for most people (see, for example, Matthew 19:4-6), and yet He suggests that some people might choose celibacy in special circumstances, but repeats that celibacy is not for everyone: "Not everyone can accept this word" (Matthew 19:11). Jesus' disciples were married, including Peter (see Matthew 8:14), who some claim was the first pope. The Christian writer Paul later picks up this idea of celibacy being a gift for some, but not to be forced on anybody because love and sexual passion can be so strong (see 1 Corinthians 7:7-9).

The early Christians also taught a positive attitude toward sex. One early writer said in about 60 AD, "Marriage should be honoured by all, and the marriage bed kept pure, for God will judge the adulterer and all the sexually immoral" (Hebrews 13:4). So, for Christians, sex outside the loving commitment of marriage is wrong, but sex within it is honourable and clean.

Temple prostitution continued into Roman times, and was a temptation to the early Christians. Paul talks straight to the Christian men in Corinth—a town where temple prostitution was common—"Do you not know that your bodies are members of Christ himself? Shall I then take the members of Christ and unite them with a prostitute? Never! Do you not know that he who unites himself with a prostitute is one with her in body? . . . But he who unites himself with the Lord is one with him in spirit. Flee from sexual immorality. All other sins a man commits are outside his body, but he who sins sexually sins against his own body. Do you not know that your body is a temple of the Holy Spirit, who is in you, whom you have received from God? You are not your own; you were bought at a price. Therefore honour God with your body" (1 Corinthians 6:15-20).

He recognises that sex can be holy and so can the body, but that wrong sex can be damaging to body and spirit. This is the original Christian teaching, long before Augustine confused it.

Is Christianity sexist?

Part of Brown's motivation in writing the book seems to be to increase the status and dignity of women. His website mentions the novel being "very empowering to women," and he writes that modern religion leaves goddesses out of the picture and so women "in most cultures have been stripped of their spiritual power."[18] He aims to bring back the idea of goddesses and "the sacred feminine" by making Mary Magdalene divine, and thus to raise the status of women.

His intentions are admirable. Increasing the dignity and respect of women would be a great thing. But Brown doesn't build a convincing case. He blames Christianity for removing the goddess so as to allow male domination: "The Priory believes that Constantine and his male successors successfully converted the world from matriarchal paganism to patriarchal Christianity by waging a campaign of propaganda that demonised the sacred feminine, obliterating the goddess from modern religion forever."[19]

Reading that comment and others in *The Da Vinci Code,* you'd think gods and goddesses kept male and female in happy harmony for all those centuries before sexist Christians came along and spoiled it all. But how does that fit with history?

It is widely acknowledged that men have been dominant for most of history. Women have been treated as the property of their husbands, and have been denied education and the right to own property, vote, speak in public meetings and many other basic human rights. This was true in the Assyrian, Babylonian, Persian, Greek and Roman empires that ruled the biblical world, and also in traditional Chinese, Indian, African and American cultures. The Greek philosopher Aristotle taught that a woman's importance was ranked somewhere between a man and a slave.[20] Sadly, this is still the situation in many countries today.

This oppression existed long before Christianity. So how is it fair to blame it on the church? And how does it help?

Part of this supposed Christian plot was suppressing the story of Mary Magdalene. Brown claims Mary was the rock on which the church was built, but that men won a power struggle and the church became male dominated, and so "the Church outlawed speaking of the shunned Mary Magdalene."[21]

It's a bizarre claim. Mary was never shunned. She was mentioned many times in the accepted Gospels. If Brown's theory is true, and sexist priests edited the Bible, how could that be explained? And countless churches have been named after her, along with elite colleges like Magdalen College, Oxford (founded in 1448), and Magdalene College, Cambridge (1428).

So that's another piece of fiction.

Goddess worship?

And goddesses were worshipped long before Christianity, but did they help the status of women?

There is no question that goddess worship existed in Old Testament times, millennia before the birth of Christ. But from the earliest times, the Bible prophets were opposed to such worship because it was part of fertility rites, and because these goddesses were just examples of humans making gods in their own image.

Ironically—as can be seen in the biblical stories—the more Israel worshipped pagan goddesses through sexualised worship, the more women were devalued as playthings. The biblical history of Judges gives one of many examples of this.

In its early chapters, when Israel is worshipping Yahweh, a woman is in the highest place. The brilliant Deborah is the national leader. In a great adventure story with strong female leads (Judges 4-5), she speaks prophetically and helps the army defeat enemy attackers, and uses the honoured title "mother in Israel" (Judges 5:7).

By the end of the book, Israel has fallen back into worship of many gods and goddesses, and the writer depicts women being pack-raped (see Judges 19) and fathers letting their daughters be kidnapped as wives for strangers, giving the girls no choice (see Judges 21:12-23). The writer's message is obvious: the true religion of Yahweh raises the dignity and respect of women, while paganism lowers it. In Deborah's words, problems arose "when they chose new gods" (Judges 5:8).

And throughout Israel's history, prophets condemned goddess worship. It was nothing to do with gender. There were false gods and goddesses. The point was that they were not the real God, and that partial worship of God was not enough to build real spirituality, ethics and success. Yet

Fertility religion?

Fertility religions saw nature as influenced by the spiritual world. Brown comes close to this idea in a few passages: "Gazing out at the rustling trees of College Garden, Langdon sensed her playful presence. The signs were everywhere. Like a taunting silhouette emerging from the fog, the branches of Britain's oldest apple tree burgeoned with five-petalled blossoms, all glistening like Venus. The goddess was in the garden now. She was dancing in the rain, singing songs of the ages, peeking out from behind the bud-filled branches as if to remind Langdon that the fruit of knowledge was growing just beyond his reach."[22] And again: "For a moment, he thought he heard a woman's voice . . . the wisdom of the ages . . . whispering up from the chasms of the earth."[23]

This is an animistic view of nature. Animism (from the Latin word *anima*, meaning "spirit") teaches that the physical world is affected by spirits.

Thus it sees nature as alive and sacred, and claims spirits can live in places, animals and plants. This can often result in nature worship, where magic and divination are used to try to get information and power from the spirit world.

Paul, the Rabbi-turned-Christian, offers a clear view of this: "For since the creation of the world God's invisible qualities—his eternal power and divine nature—have been clearly seen, being understood from what has been made, so that men are without excuse. For although they knew God, they neither glorified him as God nor gave thanks to him, but their thinking became futile and their foolish hearts were darkened. Although they claimed to be wise, they became fools and exchanged the glory of the immortal God for images made to look like mortal man and birds and animals and reptiles. Therefore God gave them over in the sinful desires of their hearts to sexual impurity for the degrading of their bodies with one another" (Romans 1:20-24).

false gods and goddesses were worshipped by Israelites who should have known better, even the once-great King Solomon (see 1 Kings 1:1-10). These religions were condemned not for the gender of their deities, but for their false ideas that ruined people's lives.

Goddesses were worshipped in Christian times as well. For example, the many-breasted goddess Diana was the patroness and pin-up girl of Ephesus, a city where the Christian apostles attracted converts and suffered mob violence (see Acts 19:23–20:1). Yet this was clearly a different religion from Christianity.

Is God male-focused?

Do the biblical religions (Judaism and Christianity) worship a male God?

No. God is Spirit. The Bible uses the word *He* to describe God because using the word *It* would sound too impersonal. And yet God also uses feminine images of Himself. God is often said to feel *rachumim,* which means "intense compassion" and the tenderest mother love, and actually comes from the Hebrew word for "womb" (see Isaiah 49:15; Deuteronomy 13:17; and many more).

Jesus appeared as a male, but used female metaphors about Himself, for example comparing His love for Jerusalem to the love of a mother hen for its young (see Matthew 23:37). Jesus treated the Samaritan woman—a foreigner from a hated nation, and a woman with a questionable sexual past—as a friend. He taught Mary just like His male disciples. After His resurrection, Jesus first appeared to women and gave women the privilege and responsibility of telling His disciples—of being apostles to the apostles. Jesus affirmed women in whatever role they chose: if they were mothers, He was not too busy to bless them and their children (see Luke 18:15–17); if they had financial and management gifts, He worked with them in leadership roles (for example, Joanna in Luke 8:3).

In the sexist world of those days, all 12 of the apostles Christ chose were men, but it would have been unfair on women to give them that role. Women's testimony was not allowed in court, and apostles had to give public testimony of Christ's resurrection. Jesus did not send women out to be shot down in that kind of battle, but He fought for their dignity indirectly and much more effectively. Within that world, Christ worked to change the status of women.

Paul summarised Christ's teaching like this: "There is neither Jew nor Greek, slave nor free, male nor female, for you are all one in Christ Jesus" (Galatians 3:28).

That is a radical, liberating statement. Brown claims "Jesus was the original feminist." There is no question Jesus was interested in a better life for both women and men—and for slaves as well—as equally deserving of happiness.

The early Christian church benefited from women in teaching and leadership roles. Paul wrote some passages that generations of male commentators have misused, but he still greets "these women who have contended at my side in the cause of the gospel, along with Clement and the rest of my fellow-workers, whose names are in the book of life" (Philippians 4:3). Women prophesied, speaking the words of God (see Acts 21:8, 9). The status of Christian women was elevated to a position of respect rarely seen in any culture.

Unfortunately, the church later copied society around it more than it copied Jesus and so the medieval church copied medieval ideas about the treatment of women. Sadly, it still does in many places today. This is an ongoing problem for the church. But it doesn't reflect on Jesus. He left a positive example. If only the church had stayed with it!

Core Christianity is about liberating men and women from inequality, and giving dignity and worth to every person equally. Christianity also makes sense as a set of ethics for living, including in what it says about our sex lives. It is neither restrictive and unbalanced—like some sections of the church—nor just fluffy talk that lets us go wherever our lusts lead us. It is balanced and sensible. If only *The Da Vinci Code* had painted this picture more accurately.

Chapter 6

THE GOSPEL OF MARY

The plot behind the plot in *The Da Vinci Code* is that Jesus married Mary Magdalene and they had a daughter, Sarah. Brown sees evidence in:

1. The art of Leonardo da Vinci

Brown believes there are hidden clues in Leonardo da Vinci's painting *The Last Supper*. He claims the figure next to Jesus is not the disciple John, but a disguised Mary Magdalene, and that this is encoded by a V-shape that symbolises the sacred feminine and the Holy Grail. Brown claims the Holy Grail is Mary herself, not a cup as is traditionally believed. But if this figure is Mary, where is the apostle John?

Yet the long-haired figure next to Christ is most likely John. He was the youngest disciple, and Renaissance art often feminised young male beauty:[1] there was a long tradition of painting John with fair skin and light or red hair.[2] For this reason and others, Brown's theory is not supported by recognised art historians.

Even if all this were in the painting, why would Leonardo da Vinci, painting in Italy in 1498, more than 1400 years after the event, know more than the eyewitnesses who wrote the Gospels? Brown claims da Vinci had special knowledge as one of the Grand Masters of the Priory of Sion, and he cites *Les Dossiers Secrets,* the documents in the Bibliotheque Nationale in Paris. The problem is that these *Dossiers* are widely regarded as 20th century forgeries.[3]

They were created by a group headed by Pierre Plantard, who was one of the founders of a club named "The Priory of Sion," registered in France in 1956. The club soon broke up, but was revived by Plantard, who made incredible claims about its ancient history. These claims were contradicted by Andre Bonhomme, the club's founding president. In the 1980s, Plantard became involved in a corruption scandal and was investigated. His house was searched and officials seized Priory of Sion documents, some claiming Plantard was actually the true king of France. Under oath, Plantard admitted he had fabricated the entire story. The judge concluded he was a harmless crank and issued a warning for "playing games."[4]

Fascinating fiction while it lasted, but no reason to rewrite history.

2. The Nag Hammadi manuscripts and Gnostic "gospels"

Brown claims that the Gnostic Gospel of Philip is evidence that Jesus and Mary Magdalene were married. He has Sophie read from it: "And the companion of the Saviour is Mary Magdalene. Christ loved her more than all the disciples and used to kiss her often on her mouth. The rest of the disciples were offended by it and expressed disapproval. They said to Him 'Why do you love her more than all of us?'"

Sophie comments that this says nothing of marriage, but Teabing counters, "As any Aramaic scholar will tell you, the word *companion*, in those days, literally meant spouse."[5]

There are several factual errors here:

1. This passage was not written in Aramaic, but in Coptic, an ancient Egyptian language, where the word "companion" (*koinonos*) simply means a friend rather than a spouse.

2. The original manuscript is so old that some words are now missing. Brown and some websites have words added by guesswork, but have not told readers this. Yet a standard reference reveals what the quotation actually says (with gaps indicated by both dots and brackets):

"And the companion of the [. . .] Mary Magdalene. [. . . loved] her more than [all] the disciples, and used to kiss her [often] on her [. . .]. The rest of [the disciples . . .]. They said to him, 'Why do you love her more than all of us?'"[6]

And so the word *mouth* is supplied—it's only a guess. It may have been hand, cheek, forehead—we just do not know. And kisses were often just a sign of friendship in that culture. Brown does not tell his readers this.

3. One would not expect to find evidence in a Gnostic gospel that Jesus was a husband and father. Gnostic gospels portray Jesus as a spiritual being and only apparently physical. And Gnostics believed that the flesh was evil. Why would a perfect spirit being engage in physical love?

4. As we have noted, the Gnostic gospels were written late (between 150 and 250 AD). It is clear the Gospel of Philip was not written by the apostle Philip, but by a later author using his name. So these "gospels" are not to be taken as history. The editor of the Nag Hammadi library, Professor James Robinson, wrote, "I think the only relevant text for historical information about Mary Magdalene is the New Testament."[7]

Bart Ehrman says, "Even if our early sources did claim that Jesus and Mary were lovers and/or married, we would have to examine these sources to see whether the claims were true. But as it turns out, Teabing's assertions notwithstanding, not a single one of our ancient sources indicates that Jesus was married, let alone married to Mary Magdalene. All such claims are part of modern fictional reconstructions of Jesus' life, not rooted in the surviving accounts themselves."[8]

3. Jewish culture

Brown claims Jewish culture condemned celibacy.[9] There is no question Jewish culture saw a loving relationship and family as one of the best gifts of God, but the historians Josephus and Philo both mention Jewish individuals who were unmarried, and Jewish groups like the Essenes actually encouraged singleness.

Brown claims Jesus must have been married or the Gospels would have mentioned His singleness, but that is an argument from silence and—as we noticed previously—Jesus described reasons why *some* would choose singleness (see Matthew 19:12).

So Brown's claims do not stack up.

Another reason: While married women were usually referred to with their husband's name—for example "Joanna, the wife of Chuza" (Luke 8:1)—Mary is never called "Mary, the wife of Jesus."

So Brown's evidence for the claim is very questionable. Dr Ben Witherington III uses the accepted Gospels as solid sources for his research. He comments, "What I would hope is that when the hullabaloo settles, it will cause people to go back and read the biblical narratives for themselves. A text without context is just a pretext for whatever you want it to be."[10]

The gospel of Mary Magdalene

Was Mary Magdalene Jesus Christ's divine lover, the first apostle, a demon-possessed prostitute or a victim of slander by jealous male priests?

There is no doubt Mary is hot news: "In an era when 'God talk' has moved convincingly into the media/entertainment arena, observers say, her story is captivating because it encapsulates major unresolved issues facing Christianity—the role of women in the church, the place of human sexuality and the yearning for the feminine aspect of the Divine."[11]

For centuries, Mary has appeared topless or seductively clothed in paintings by the masters, usually with red hair and an alabaster jar of perfumed oil. She was the prostitute in *Jesus Christ Superstar*, singing "I don't know how to love him." She was a constant sexual temptation in *The Last Temptation of Christ*. In Cecil B De Mille's silent classic *King of Kings*—often rerun as Easter TV—she is a bejewelled courtesan with pet leopards and male slaves. She's mentioned in *The Magdalene Sisters,* a movie about Ireland's grim institutions where girls who got "into trouble" with pregnancy or rebelliousness were locked up by their parents to work in laundries, often bullied and abused by nuns. Mary the ex-prostitute was the example, the bad girl who came good.

Brown's novel depicts her as the lover of Jesus Christ, the divine Holy Grail herself, who escaped to France with His daughter, Sarah. Brown claims sexist churchmen covered up this truth, and tarred Mary's reputation by making up the story of prostitution. Brown uses this to argue for a gender-equal spirituality and the "sacred feminine," the female side of God.

Arguing for equality is commendable, but Brown needs to make the case on solid ground. Few historians take his story seriously.

Churches today are re-examining their ancient texts and finding in them much more evidence for gender equality. As part of this, many churches welcome women into ministry and so they are asking whether Mary was the earliest female minister and apostle. The Gospels certainly depict her as the first person to announce that Christ had risen, which makes her an apostle to the apostles.

This important female role was very likely downplayed by the more sexist church of later centuries.

Some scholars claim that sexist churchmen weakened Mary's credibility by falsely labelling her a prostitute, a title not given her in the Gospels. They claim that Mary was first called a prostitute in 591 AD, when a sermon by Pope Gregory confused her story with that of an unnamed female "sinner" in Luke 7.

After 1400 years, the Roman Catholic Church changed its view in 1969, stating that Mary was not a prostitute. And since then, many scholars have viewed her as a wealthy woman, perhaps married, who befriended Jesus and supported Him financially.

Yet recent scholars of the calibre of John Wenham and Andre Feuillet see clues in the Gospels that Mary was a prostitute. There is evidence that three Gospel writers covered up the identity of a woman with a sinful past, and only John, writing in later years, reveals her name as Mary. This Mary, living in Bethany, could have been the same person as Mary "Magdalene," meaning from Magdala. Magdala was a wealthy town criticised by the rabbis for its moral "wickedness," so a girl going there to work in prostitution would fit the picture. They also quote the Gospel statements that Mary Magdalene had a very dark past, including demonic possession (see Mark 16:9; Luke 8:2).[12] (For a discussion of this evidence, please see Appendix B.)

Yet to see Mary as an ex-prostitute is not to shame or discredit her. In fact it discovers an inspiring story of a woman rising from a rough background to an honoured role, helped by her friendship with Christ.

Would Christ welcome an ex-prostitute onto His ministry team? He did say prostitutes were going into heaven ahead of some priests because they believed and repented (see Matthew 21:31, 32). Should a past as a prostitute disqualify somebody from Christian service? Some may think so, but let's remember that Jesus' main message was about forgiveness and life-change. And the male apostles had obviously sinful pasts—Peter by publicly denying Christ (see Matthew 26:69-75), and Paul by violently attacking Christians.

Paul later wrote, "How thankful I am to Christ Jesus our Lord for . . . appointing me to serve him, even though I used to scoff at the name of

Christ. I hunted down his people. . . . But God had mercy on me . . . so that Christ Jesus could use me as a prime example of his great patience with even the worst sinners. Then others will realise that they, too, can believe in him and receive eternal life" (1 Timothy 1:12-16, NLT).

If God could use the apostle Paul to show His great patience in changing the lives of the worst sinners, then why not a prostitute?

The plot thickens

There are some great stories recorded in the Gospels about Mary of Bethany and Mary Magdalene. If they are one and the same person, then hers is an epic story. In one lifetime, Mary was:

> ▶ a sexually scarred person who knew Jesus' ability to deeply heal sin, and to meet emotional needs;
> ▶ a victim of demon possession who felt Jesus' power over the spirit world;
> ▶ a close friend to Jesus, who sat at His feet and listened by the hour to His extraordinary teaching;
> ▶ an eyewitness to a stunning miracle when her brother, Lazarus, dead for days, was resurrected;
> ▶ a coworker and financial backer of Jesus' ministry team;
> ▶ a giver, whose costly present and spontaneous tears expressed her love and gratitude;
> ▶ a listener, who heard more clearly than most disciples that Jesus would die—and that it was to save humans from sin;
> ▶ an eyewitness to His death;
> ▶ a witness to where He was buried;
> ▶ the first human to see Jesus after He resurrected;
> ▶ the first to tell others that He had beaten death—and the first preacher of the Resurrection to be doubted and disbelieved!

What a life! Far from demeaning this woman, it turns her into someone whose story would be told worldwide and in every age, alongside Jesus' own story.

Mary was a close friend of Jesus, a statement about how God values women, and "Exhibit A" of Jesus' ability to do positive things with people, despite their past mistakes.

Let's now look at the story in more detail.

Mary's story

When she first met Jesus, Mary Magdalene was in serious trouble. She was possessed by seven demons until Jesus exorcised demons from her (see Mark 16:9; Luke 8:2). This may sound like a plot from *Charmed, Medium, Ghost Whisperer* or some other TV show, but occult phenomena like these are taken seriously today by many modern researchers in parapsychology. Some scholars see this as a prescientific attempt to describe mental illness, or some kind of metaphor,[13] but Jesus seems to take it seriously as spiritual warfare. He often mentions "the devil" and "Satan" and his demons. Evil spirits are said to be "unclean," and to cause madness and destruction (see Mark 5:1-13). Jesus said He made demons leave "by the Spirit of God" (see Matthew 12:28; Luke 4:33-36), so there is a war going on: Jesus bringing God's kingdom to earth under attack from Satan, the self-styled "prince of this world," whom Jesus came to throw out and to judge (see John 12:31; 16:11). Driving out demons from the human psyche was one of the ways Jesus showed that His kingdom was going to replace human sickness, sin and despair with wellness, peace and joy. It was a "head-on collision" between "the kingdom of Satan and the kingdom of God,"[14] and showed God's kingdom was more powerful (see Luke 11:20).

Jesus also warned that when He had driven out one demon from a person, they must allow God's Spirit to fill them or else the demon can bring back seven others (see Luke 10:24-26; Matthew 12:43-45). So Mary's "seven demons" may suggest a story of being freed from her possession, then making bad choices and falling back into possession even more severely. This would mean Jesus had to show incredible patience and determination to help her turn her life around, giving her time to try, fail and try again as many times as it took. In the end, she won—with a lot of help from Jesus.

The Gospels do not give much detail at all on her career, except to say that she was a "sinner" in that city (see Luke 7:37), which in that culture suggests a local prostitue.[15] After her change of heart and occupation, Mary Magdalene worked on Jesus' mission team. As He travelled around teaching and healing, Mary and several other women supported Him in key financial-management roles. These women worked with Jesus and financially supported him (Luke 8:2, 3).

Snappy sister, resurrected brother

Jesus also enjoyed the company of Mary's family. While travelling through Bethany, He was invited into the family home by Martha, Mary's sister. Martha was a driven person, stressed by trying to serve up a feast for Jesus and a dozen hungry disciples. Meanwhile Mary was simply enjoying Jesus' company and teaching, sitting at His feet in the humble position of a learner.[16]

A stressed Martha burst into the room and snapped, "Lord, don't you care that my sister has left me to do the work by myself? Tell her to help me!" You can hear the hurt and anger.

Jesus answered, "Martha, Martha"—saying her name twice perhaps to slow things down and make her take a breath, becoming more self-aware. Then He acknowledged her stress, but suggested a healthier choice: "You are worried and upset about many things. But only one thing is needed. Mary has chosen what is better, and it will not be taken away from her" (Luke 10:38-42).

Jesus was not encouraging laziness, but balance. Drive and work are good, but not without time to relax with friends and, above all, for intimate communication with God.

John also tells the story of Lazarus of Bethany, brother to Mary and Martha and a good friend of Jesus. Lazarus became seriously sick, and the sisters sent a message to let Jesus know, hoping He would come and heal him. Jesus told His disciples, "This sickness will not end in death," and did not go to Bethany until days later. By that time Lazarus was dead, which must have made the disciples wonder whether their Messiah prophet was wrong.

When Jesus arrived, the sisters wanted to see Him. Martha—a dominant, logical personality—marched out to see Him and said, "Lord, if you had been here, my brother would not have died. But I know that even now God will give you whatever you ask."

Jesus offered her solid assurance: "Your brother will rise again."

Martha answered, "I know he will rise again in the resurrection at the last day."[17]

But Jesus responded, "I am the resurrection and the life. He who believes in me will live, even though he dies. . . . Do you believe this?" (John 11:26). He was able to appeal to Martha's intellect with a faith based on solid reasoning.

She said, "Yes, Lord. I believe that you are the Christ, the Son of God, who was to come into the world."

And then she called Mary—a more emotional personality—who had been waiting in the house. When she saw Jesus, she fell at His feet and said the same thing as her sister, but probably in a softer, more tearful voice: "Lord, if you had been here, my brother would not have died."

Jesus had heard her wailing. He did not present facts to her, but asked her to show Him the grave. And then He simply cried with her. He gave her what she needed most at that time—sympathy, empathy, understanding.

And then He showed that He was also God Almighty. He stepped up to the tomb, which was cut into rock, and told people to roll away the stone from the entrance. Martha bluntly protested because a four-day-old corpse would smell. Jesus gave her tough logic again: "Did I not tell you that if you believed, you would see the glory of God?" She did not argue, and so they rolled away the stone.

And the dead Lazarus came back to life.

Mary's reaction is not recorded—but you can guess.

She showed her love

Shortly before His death, "Jesus arrived at Bethany, where Lazarus lived, whom Jesus had raised from the dead. Here a dinner was given in Jesus' honour. Martha served, while Lazarus was among those . . . at the table with him" (John 12:1, 2). There is no mention of Mary being invited, in fact she seems to arrive while they are eating, perhaps sneaking into the house. It was springtime, so the house may have been left open to let in cool air.

The host was Simon the Pharisee, a member of a hardline traditional religious group, who no doubt regarded Mary as a great "sinner" and may not have wanted her in his house. Yet Simon is also called a "leper" (see Matthew 26:6; Mark 14:3), and lepers were considered contagious and banned from any social contact. So Simon must have been one of the many lepers healed by Jesus, because by the time of this story he was able to see people again.[18]

The Pharisees taught that any sickness was a judgment of God for their sin (compare John 9:2), so Simon's diagnosis as a leper must have been a double tragedy—a sign that his life was practically over and that God was cursing him. So when Jesus healed him, it was more than physical health—it was a sign that God loved him and forgave his sin.

After that, you would think Simon would have understood God's unconditional love and grace, but somehow he reserved that for himself and treated Mary as undeserving. Perhaps he felt he deserved to be loved and forgiven because he was basically a good person. Yet Jesus was about to show him how wide God's love is. Luke's account calls Mary a sinner three times—but Luke emphasises three times that Jesus is able to forgive sins.[19]

Mary was in the room, probably secretly, listening to Jesus teach. The guests were not seated, but were lying Roman-style on couches or mats around a low table, with their heads facing each other and their feet pointing out. John describes the scene: "Then Mary took about a pint of pure nard, an expensive perfume; she poured it on Jesus' feet and wiped his feet with her hair. And the house was filled with the fragrance of the perfume" (John 12:3).

Nard is a perfume extracted from the spike of the nard plant, which grows near the foothills of the Himalayas. It had probably come via the spice markets of India by ship to Arabia, then by camel train to Jerusalem. It was extremely exotic and this nard was pure, not mixed with cheaper substances. It cost a year's wages for a working person. One can only imagine how much soul-destroying work it would take for a prostitute to earn this.

Two Gospel writers—Mark and John—tell us that she anointed Jesus' head with this perfumed oil. This was fairly standard hospitality for guests in the ancient world, where oil was commonly used for personal grooming, something like cologne, face cream and hair-care products in our culture (see Luke 7:46; see also Psalm 23:5; 133:1, 2). But anointing is especially what happened to a king, in fact the word *Messiah*—the Jewish name for God's chosen king—comes from the word *mashach*, meaning "to anoint with oil." The title "Christ" means the same thing in Greek. So this could be seen as Mary's statement that she believed Jesus was the Messiah.

Two Gospel writers—Luke and John—tell us she also anointed

His feet. The only time that was done in that culture was as a funeral ritual.[20] The respected Roman Catholic scholar Raymond Brown writes: "One does not anoint the feet of a living person, but one might anoint the feet of a corpse as part of the ritual of preparing the whole body for burial."[21] This is why John records the strange detail of Jesus' feet being anointed.

It was also a Jewish tradition that when you anointed a dead person, you broke the neck of the ointment bottle—perhaps as a symbol that it would not be used again, or a sign of loss—and later put the bottle into their burial cask.[22] This is why Mary broke the box, even though it was made of expensive alabaster (see Mark 14:3). Jesus recognised what the symbol meant: "She poured perfume on my body beforehand to prepare for my burial" (Mark 14:8).

Jesus had often told His disciples He would die by crucifixion, but mostly they did not listen or understand. Sometimes they even argued with Him about it, because they believed Messiah would be an invincible king and would live forever, and His death did not fit their plans (see Matthew 16:21-23). Jesus was trying to make them understand that He had to die for the sins of the world; this was His main mission. But while the other disciples seemed slow to understand, Mary got the point that Jesus would actually die.

He was dying to pay for the forgiveness of human sin, including hers. She had listened better and understood Him better than His disciples did. No doubt the thought of His death was sad for her. And so she decided to show her love while He was still alive rather than wait until He was dead.

"What she has done will be told"

The extravagant gift was a spontaneous thankyou. Mary was probably trying to be unobtrusive. But then the tears came. If tears can be explained in words, then these ones spoke of love, thanks, regret and happiness, and of missing Him before He even died. She hadn't planned on tears, and as they rained onto His dusty feet and made a drippy mess on the floor, she had nothing to wipe them up, so she unwound her long hair and dabbed blindly at His feet.

This only added to the scandal. The natural beauty of a woman's hair was considered by some to be too seductive to be shown in public. To have an ex-prostitute unfurl her long, flowing hair and touch you looked highly suggestive. It seemed like unthinkable defilement for a Pharisee. And while Mary was at Jesus' feet, she began to kiss them, a cultural sign of "affectionate gratitude."[23]

At this point Luke lets us inside the head of Simon the Pharisee. (Luke was not an eyewitness, and may have interviewed Simon about it later.) Simon was silently wondering if Jesus was a prophet or just a dangerous fanatic as most Pharisees believed. Simon expected a real prophet would know enough to reject this "sinful" woman. That was what Simon himself would have done.

Yet Jesus was about to show Simon that He could read his unspoken thoughts—and that He knew exactly who Mary was. He told him a story about two people in debt, and how the person forgiven the larger debt feels more gratitude and love. Jesus was politely telling Simon that both he and Mary had been in debt to God, but had been forgiven freely. Neither could pay. Both depended totally on God's kindness to save them, and neither had any basis to feel better than the other. And the more a person realises how deeply they need grace, the more they will love God.

Jesus also contrasted Mary's actions with Simon's half-hearted hospitality. It was expected in that culture that a visitor would be given water to wash their feet after walking on dusty roads behind animals, and oil to freshen up their hair and face, and a formal kiss of greeting. Simon had not given Jesus any of these, because he was still half-hearted and judgmental about the Man who had healed him from leprosy. Simon was the classic smug religionist who was spiritually blind. Yet Mary's heart religion led her to generosity and lavish love.

Simon's religion had no place for Mary, and "no real answer to the problem of sin." It could only condemn her. "But Jesus could actually do away with sin, and in this deepest sense bring salvation and peace."[24] Jesus told Mary her faith—the simple belief in the love of Jesus and the forgiveness He would buy with His death—had saved her. He said she could go in peace. This was not telling her to leave, but was a Jewish saying to wish someone peace and happiness.

God was on her side. Why would she care who was against her?

Criticism

Then out of nowhere came a public attack. A disciple, Judas Iscariot, objected: "Why wasn't this perfume sold and the money given to the poor? It was worth a year's wages" (John 12:5).

The comment persuaded the other disciples, probably because Jesus so often emphasised the duty to help poorer people and had even told one terminally selfish rich man to sell all his assets and give to the poor (see Matthew 11:5; 19:21). Yet even in a needy world there is a need to show love extravagantly. This was a classic case of putting money behind emotional intelligence and spiritual understanding.

"Leave her alone," Jesus replied—a fairly gentle rebuke considering how this mind-reader could have exposed Judas' own theft from the charity bag. "It was intended that she should save this perfume for the day of my burial. You will always have the poor among you, but you will not always have me" (John 12:7). He was not saying helping the poor didn't matter—in fact He was reminding them of an earlier Bible text written by Moses: "There will always be poor people. . . . Therefore I command you to be open-handed . . . towards the poor and needy" (Deuteronomy 15:11).

So when smug religionists attacked Mary, Jesus was proud of her. When some men missed the depth of her heart, Jesus said that wherever His story was told, hers would be told as well: "I tell you the truth, wherever this gospel is preached throughout the world, what she has done will also be told, in memory of her" (Matthew 26:13). She had understood Jesus' death and offered her memorial to Him;[25] He made her immortal and unforgettable. Her story shows how belief in Jesus brings forgiveness, spiritual freshness and a new beginning.

She saw His death

When Jesus was to be publicly executed, Mary came to offer her support. Most of His male disciples had "deserted him and fled" (Matthew 26:56), afraid to appear in public in case the Roman soldiers had orders to arrest His followers too. But Mary and some other women took the risk of being at His crucifixion (see Matthew 27:55, 56).

She watched His kindness to others when He was in agony. She saw that He didn't curse the Roman soldiers as they drove great nails into His body. She saw the earthquake as He died, as if nature were protesting and the earth grinding its teeth. She heard the Roman centurion supervising the execution finally say, "Surely this man was the Son of God!" (Mark 15:39).

When His body was taken off the cross, wrapped in clean linen, and laid in a borrowed tomb, Mary Magdalene stayed there watching with another woman named Mary, the wife of Clopas. Then she went home to spend the saddest Sabbath of her life. Her friend, her healer, her God in human form, had been taken away. Perhaps her only comfort was that she had shown her love while He was alive—and the fact that she had already seen one resurrection.

When the Sabbath was over, at dawn on Sunday morning, Mary Magdalene and "the other Mary"—the wife of Clopas (John 19:25)—came to the sepulchre to anoint Jesus' body (Mark 16:1).

But they were too late—He was alive.

They had been wondering how they would move the stone, but they found that an angel had already done that job for them (see Matthew 28:2). Mary went into the tomb weeping, as she had at her brother's tomb (see John 20:11; compare 11:31-35). Angels asked her why she was weeping, and she must not have been seeing clearly, because she told them someone had taken away her Lord. Then she walked out of the tomb and almost bumped into Jesus. He had chosen to see her first, before any other person. She was still weeping, and He asked her why. Again He was sympathetic to her grief.

She thought He was the gardener, and asked where Jesus' body was.

Jesus then said her name in the language of her heart, their native Hebrew: *Mariam!*

She instantly replied in Hebrew: *Rabbouni!* The word means rabbi or teacher, but the ending is personal and endearing,[26] something like calling a friendly teacher "Prof." It is respectful of His role, but shows they are friends. Jesus is balancing the authority and power of being God and also the intimacy and empathy of being a human.

Jesus had also said to her, "Who is it you are looking for?" (John 20:15). This is the question He asked His disciples when He first called them to follow Him and work with Him. And they answered *"Rabbouni"* as well, and then became His apostles (see John 1:35-40).[27] And now Jesus asked

Mary to be an apostle to the apostles—to go and tell them He was alive again as He promised. And so Mary was the first witness to the fact of Jesus' resurrection.

A woman was the first person to announce the staggering news that Jesus had defeated death. Yet here's the irony. When Mary and the other women went and told the apostles He was alive, the men "did not believe the women, because their words seemed to them like nonsense" (Luke 24:11). "In the cultural stereotypes of the day . . . these are 'only women,' not to be believed in matters of deep importance. Their report is passed off as hysteria. . . . Though Luke has a high view of women, he reflects here his awareness of the widespread tendency to discount the word of a woman."[28]

But if the church had embarrassing moments of sexism, Jesus never did. He later appeared in person and powerfully confirmed what the women had said.

Witherington points out that Jesus chose Mary to be the first to announce His resurrection. His conclusion: "Since she was commissioned by Jesus to be in essence an apostle to the apostles, she provided the most crucial precedent in the New Testament for women to be teachers, preachers or evangelists."[29]

Jesus and Mary

For Brown, casting Mary Magdalene as a prostitute would demean her sacred feminine nature. But the Gospels show a picture that honours this woman, and turns a rough past into a golden future.

This story by no means puts Mary down. She is one of Christ's best friends, a disciple of whom Christ was most proud, and one of the best examples of what He came to do.

Chapter 7

RIGHT OR WRONG?
LET'S MAKE A BET

W hat if we're wrong?

We have shown that the Gospels are written by sane eyewitnesses with no reason to lie. We've demonstrated that the Gospels have not been changed—there are too many manuscript copies too close to the event. We've seen strong historical evidence that Jesus Christ was crucified then came back to life, and Christian, Jewish and Roman historians confirm various parts of this story. We've seen striking evidence of superhuman ability to predict the future, and of the importance of Jesus in a credible ancient prophecy. We've also seen that original Christian teaching makes a lot of sense about sexuality, and also promotes gender equality.

But what if we're wrong? What if Jesus Christ was a fictional character invented by people who couldn't handle the fact that life is short, cruel and meaningless, and who needed to believe there was an Imaginary Friend up there to protect them? What if we humans really are only the product of chance chemical reactions and random mutations? What if we die and become nothing more than carbon compounds, with no chance of survival in any form? What if there is no ultimate right and wrong, no big truths, no point to living, no afterlife?

If that's true, we will all die one day and never wake up. But what will we have missed by believing in Jesus? We will have lived our lives—about 28,000 days of them, on average—believing we are loved deeply. We will have spent our days inspired by an extremely likeable character—

one of the most influential in all literature—and been challenged to live generously and to treat others as we like to be treated. We will have felt secure enough to look our personal faults in the eye and try to overcome them, while always feeling the grace and approval of God. We will have been optimists: in worrying and painful times, we will have trusted that we are being looked after by God, and will have stayed calmer than we could have on our own. We will have had a great cause to save us from self-centredness and selfishness, and bring out our passionate best for other people.

We will have looked forward to life in a perfect place, where God has eradicated pain, suffering and evil and we can have fun with people we love. We will have stood at the funerals of our loved ones saying, "See you later," and actually meant it, our sorrow tinged with hope. We will of course have to put up with hard times and loss—but we believe Christ will give back even more (see Mark 10:29, 30). Some Christians will have lost their lives for their faith, whether in the Colosseum or in a modern state without religious freedom—but in countless stories they face death with a calm dignity envied by their killers. And everyone faces death sometime.

We may have passed up a few "gratifications" that are short-term and risky anyway. But on balance our lives will have been happier. Then we'll sleep forever in the cemetery alongside everyone else. What have we lost?

But what if we're right? What if one day we will wake up in a place that is perfect one day and better the next? What if we wake up in a perfect body, that never aches, ages or dies—or even needs to sleep (see Revelation 21:4, 25; 22:5)? What if we wake up with every other seeker after truth and love, knowing God's ability to transform a human heart and realise our full potential, so we're living among the very best human beings from every age? And what if we just keep on getting happier, wiser and more stimulated by the incredible creativity of God so we never want life to stop—and it never does?

We will have gained an eternity. If we hadn't believed, we would have had nothing, or less than nothing.

Do the maths: an infinite amount of happiness verses a zero or a negative.

Believe:	Possible upside: eternity of bliss, infinite pay-off
	Possible downside: almost nothing
Don't believe:	Possible upside: gratifications? (debatable)
	Possible downside: miss out on a perfect life in a perfect world that lasts forever

The consequences of this choice are astronomically, enormously, infinitely, gigagasaurously important. (That's big.)

What do you think?

A.   Jesus was barking mad and His ideas still only appeal to dangerous nutters.

B.   Jesus was dreaming but was a harmless fanatic and maybe even inspiring.

C.   Jesus might well have been right. I'd like to see more evidence.

D.   Jesus was right.

If you chose A or B, we can still be friends and have stimulating conversations from our differing points of view. But we might cheekily ask you for a better explanation of the hardcore evidence of prophecy and history in the preceding chapters.

If you chose C, check out our websites www.davincidecode.net and www.bigquestions.com

If you chose D, read on.

Where to from here?

Well, eternal life, actually.

Meanwhile, here are some practical steps that Jesus taught.

1. Believe God knows you personally—your name and address, your dreams, your fears, your talents, the story of that person who hurt you, that choice you still regret, that dodgy thing with the money, your wish to change the world for the better. Jesus said, "Are not two sparrows sold for a penny? Yet not one of them will fall to the ground apart from the will of your Father. And even the very hairs of your head are all numbered.

So don't be afraid; you are worth more than many sparrows" (Matthew 10:29-31). You are known and valued.

Jesus also said, "The Father himself loves you" (John 16:27). Apologies to anyone who has bad experiences with the word *love*—you might add your own word: *cares for, feels for, is crazy about, likes, approves of.*

Some people question whether God loves them because they've suffered. Why didn't God help? That's a great question that deserves a complex answer, but for now we'd have to say that Christ's own life was extremely tough—born in a shed, parents ran as refugees, grew up poor, faced malicious gossip and was stalked by corrupt authorities and was eventually killed violently. He had it as tough as anyone even though He was God in the flesh. So we can be sure He understands our problems. And we can be sure that pain in our lives doesn't mean we're forgotten.

2. Step into the light. It's easy to say "Seek the truth," but many people don't actually want truth. As one comedian put it, "I have abandoned the search for truth and am looking for a good fantasy."[1]

The truth can be scary. The problem is that the truth about me cuts across my smug view of myself. I am not perfect. I have faults my friends see and faults only I know about. My love is tainted with selfishness, my kindest actions riddled with pride. I am flawed. Sure, there are people I can compare myself to and feel better than. But when I compare myself to Jesus—unstoppably kind, even to His enemies—I look pretty shabby. In fact that's one reason Jesus was and is so unpopular: we can't feel smug around Him. He shatters our self-congratulation. He knew this, because He said, "This is the verdict: Light has come into the world, but men loved darkness instead of light because their deeds were evil. Everyone who does evil hates the light, and will not come into the light for fear that his deeds will be exposed. But whoever lives by the truth comes into the light, so that it may be seen plainly that what he has done has been done through God" (John 3:19-21).

Do you want the truth? Do you want the truth about yourself? The truth is we're all sinners—and we don't naturally know it. Sin involves a separation from God and we sinners do not naturally understand God's goodness and don't feel the need for His love. Our hearts are numb. Our spirits are tone-deaf to the music and our lives can't dance to its rhythm (see Matthew 11:15-17). There's a whole spiritual world going on around us. It's as real as radio waves, yet we don't have our aerials up and we go through life missing it. And that type of ignorance is eventually fatal.

Unless we see a glimpse of light.

We may see it dimly and without focus at first. If we ignore it, it fades. If we watch it and walk toward it, it becomes clearer. As we approach it, we see wrinkles and ugliness in ourselves that the best make-up and Hollywood lighting couldn't cover. And we have a choice. Run away, comfortable in the dark until the light goes out in our lives. Or step into the light and admit we need help. Beneath our politeness, popularity, social class, education and life experience, there is an inner neediness and shabbiness that we alone can't seem to help.

"I need help, God!"

There, that wasn't so hard, was it?

3. Accept help. The major way God sent help to the human race was through Jesus Christ.

First, He became a human and lived a perfect life. And we mean perfect. While they were nailing Him to the cross, He was praying for the soldiers who did it. As you read the Gospels, you see stunning truth and impressive love in an almost impossible combination.

Second, He died for us—for the human race. It was the greatest swap in history. He died the death that our sins deserved so we could live forever. Jesus "lay down his life for his friends" (John 15:13).

You could say Jesus was absorbing the fatal consequences of human sin, personally becoming the toxic waste dump for human guilt and shame, letting us walk away clean. God Himself was solving our problem.

Or you could say He was paying the damage bill for the sins of the world. He got our bill, and we got His enormous bank balance.

But here's the toughest thing of all to believe: You don't have to earn it. You can't pay Him back, even if you lived five lifetimes as Mother Teresa nursing the poor in the slums of Calcutta. God just paid. You get it free—or not at all.

This is hard to accept. Our egos get in the way—either saying we don't need forgiveness because we're no worse than anyone else, or saying we can be good enough to repay God for some of this. This can be especially hard for people with a religious background because they think it's all about being good, when it's really about accepting help.

But all we need to do is accept it. How hard will it be for you to simply say: "Thanks, God. I want that"? What would happen if you did?

Jesus said, "If anyone loves me, he will obey my teaching. My Father will love him, and we will come to him and make our home with him" (John 14:23). So the more you come to admire Jesus, the more you start living life in the light of His teaching, because God lives with you. God is omnipresent, which means everywhere—but Jesus said God would live with us. That means God would come in Spirit-form and would become part of our lives, living within our hearts and minds. That's a fascinating, mystical truth that you can only really understand by experience. Jesus said the Spirit of God acted like the wind—you couldn't see it, but you could certainly see the changes it brought (see John 3:8). If God moves into your life, it can only be called life-changing.

Jesus said, "God so loved the world that he gave his one and only Son, that whoever believes in him shall not perish but have eternal life" (John 3:16). This is the most famous Bible text for good reason. It answers a lot of questions:

Who did Jesus come to help? The text says the whole wide world.

Who can believe in Him? Anyone. Not everyone will, but anyone can.

What are the two possible futures? Perish—as in eternal death. Or eternal life.

What do I have to do if I want eternal life? Believe in Jesus.

What if I have sinned really badly? The next verse says, "God did not send his Son into the world to condemn the world, but to save the world through him" (John 3:17). He's not here to judge but to help.

What if I don't believe? The next verse says, "Whoever does not believe stands condemned already because he has not believed in the name of God's one and only Son" (John 3:18).

And this text is not dooming people who've only just heard this. There are some good solid reasons why you might struggle to believe in Jesus. You might have been taught a scary, hardline, hateful mix-up of Christianity. You might have seen His so-called followers doing terrible things—priests abusing children, "Christians" killing Jews or just being terrible spouses, workmates or neighbours. You may have been brought up in another religion or told there was no God. Even if you do believe, it may be with 51 per cent of your head, while 49 per cent of your head has huge doubts. You may not have been shown the evidence until now. And that is totally fair and understandable. God gives people enough time and evidence to believe. Jesus is not suggesting you are a lost cause.

But Jesus is saying that how we respond to Him is important. If God shows Himself to the world by Jesus, and if I reject Jesus, then I'm rejecting God.

So if all that made sense, you may want to talk to God along the following lines:

"Hello, God. I think You love me and have a fantastic plan for my life, although I admit I've made mistakes and I need Your help. I hear that Jesus' death was to pay for my mistakes, and I'd like to accept that offer. And I'd like Your help in living my life from this point."

If you just prayed that, you're a Christian. You might want to start getting some support and advice from other Christians. We're not claiming perfection or sainthood, but we can encourage you with our own experience and help you understand the Bible and read it for yourself.

Brown's website says he wrote his novel to "serve as an open door for readers to begin their own explorations and rekindle their interest in topics of faith." If you've gotten this far, that may not be exactly what he intended, but we're sure that somewhere unseen, the totally real, totally divine Jesus Christ is smiling.

DANIEL 9: DIGGING DEEPER

"Seventy weeks are determined for your people and for your holy city, to finish the transgression, to make an end of sins, to make reconciliation for inquity, to bring in everlasting righteousness, to seal up vision and prophecy, and to annoint the Most Holy. Know therefore and understand, that from the going forth of the command to restore and build Jerusalem until Messiah the Prince, there shall be seven weeks and sixty-two weeks; the street shall be built again, and the wall, even in troublesome times. And after the sixty-two weeks Messiah shall be cut off, but not for himself; and the people of the prince who is to come shall destroy the city and the sanctuary" (Daniel 9:24-26, NKJV).

The summary:

In 539 BC, Daniel predicted that the Messiah would arrive 483 years after "the command to restore and build Jerusalem." This order came in 457 BC. And Jesus made His public appearance 483 years later in 27 AD, when He was baptised. Daniel also predicted Messiah would die—which can be dated to 31 AD—and that Jerusalem would be destroyed again—the Romans did that in 70 AD.

So what?

1. This is strong evidence for the existence of a personal God. What human could see the future more than 500 years ahead?

2. It suggests this God is caring enough to offer this type of guidance to the human race.

3. This God is involved with Jesus Christ. It becomes obvious the life and death of Jesus are important events to the human race.

The starting point of the time period

The prediction calls this "the decree to rebuild and restore Jerusalem." You might wonder which rebuilding this refers to as Jerusalem has been destroyed so many times. But obviously this refers to the decree issued just after Daniel's time, and there is no lack of historical records to pinpoint this date.

The historical books of *Ezra* and *Nehemiah* record four relevant decrees:

1. In 538/37 BC, King Cyrus of Persia gave the Jews permission to return home and rebuild their temple with money he donated—but this did not include rebuilding the city, with its defensive walls etc, and enemies from Samaria stopped them completing even the Temple (see Ezra 1:2-4).

2. In 520/519 BC, Darius I Hystaspes decreed that they could rebuild their Temple (see Ezra 6:1-12)—but still not the city.

3. The third decree was given personally by King Artaxerxes to the Jewish leader Ezra in 457 BC, allowing him to appoint public officials, use money from the king's treasury, establish Jewish law and do whatever he needed to do (see Ezra 7:18)—and so he began rebuilding the city. (The decree is recorded in Ezra 7:12-26).

4. After political pressure from the enemies of Jerusalem, King Artaxerxes stopped the rebuilding of the city until further notice (see Ezra 4:13-23). Nothing happened for 13 years until the king's Jewish cupbearer, Nehemiah, personally asked permission to go and restart the reconstruction of the city (Nehemiah 2:1-5).

So the decree that really began the rebuilding was the third one.

When did it happen? Ezra 7:8 records that "Ezra arrived in Jerusalem in the fifth month of the seventh year of the king." And we have firm dates for Artaxerxes's reign, recorded by the Greek historian Herodotus, the Alexandrian astronomer Ptolemy ("Ptolemy's Canon"), from Babylonian records, and from some records that compare Egyptian dates with the Persian–Babylonian calendar.[1] So a strong case can be made for 457 BC as the date of Artaxerxes' decree to rebuild Jerusalem. This is the starting point for Daniel's prophetic period.

The "weeks"

The "weeks" mean seven-year periods. (The New International Version of the Bible translates the word as "sevens.") Jewish law provided that the people should not work their land every seventh year, and eat only what grew naturally. This was to allow family time and relaxation, and to stop environmental damage caused by overfarming.

"For six years sow your fields, and for six years prune your vineyards and gather their crops. But in the seventh year the land is to have a sabbath of rest, a sabbath to the Lord. . . . The land is to have a year of rest. Whatever the land yields during the sabbath year will be food for you" (Leviticus 25:3-6).

This is also mentioned in the Mishna, which was written in 200 AD but recorded Jewish law from as far back as 450 BC.[2]

Biblical law also made every 50th year (after seven periods of seven years) into a special "Jubilee" event when people who had gone bankrupt and sold their land actually had it returned (see Leviticus 25:8-13). It's a fascinating idea, and has motivated the Christians who initiated the Drop the Debt campaign in the lead-up to 2000.

Jewish and Christian scholars "have understood the weeks of Daniel as weeks of years," writes Jacques Doukhan, citing a huge list. From Hellenistic literature: the Book of Jubilees (3rd/2nd century BC), the Testament of Levi (1st century BC), 1 Enoch (2nd century BC); from the Qumran collection: 11Q Melchitsedeq, 4Q 384-390 Pseudo-Ezekiel, the Damascus Document; from rabbinical literature: Seder Olam (2nd century AD), the Talmud, the Midrash Rabbah; and work from Middle Ages exegetes like Saadia Gaon, Ibn Ezre in the Miqraoth Gdoloth, and the great Rashi.[3]

Some scholars have argued the "weeks" mean seven-day weeks, but that amounts to only about a year-and-a-half and Jewish records show that rebuilding the city took longer than that, let alone all the other predictions.[4]

So 69 x 7 years = 483 years.

Was Jesus a historical figure?

Many historians do not believe Jesus was God, but almost all believe He was a real person of history, as we have already seen.

Was Jesus the Jewish Messiah?

This prophecy ends with the appearance of the "Anointed One" (in Hebrew, "Messiah," or in Greek, the "Christ"). The coming of this Messiah-king was a Jewish hope for centuries, and many Jews, including many priests (see Acts 6:7), came to believe Jesus was indeed the Messiah. The first Christians were almost all from a Jewish background, and in the two millennia since then, countless Jewish people have come to recognise Jesus as their Messiah.

Yet many Jewish leaders rejected Jesus as a false Messiah, and today people of the Jewish faith do not recognise Jesus as Messiah. Why not?

Rabbi Yechiel Eckstein writes, in *What Christians Should Know About Jews and Judaism*, that Jews expect the Messiah to bring about world peace, according to their understanding of prophecy, and Jesus did not do this. He explains, "Not only were the biblical prophecies foretelling the dawn of world peace and political harmony unfulfilled, quite the opposite occurred—Jews lost sovereignty over the land of Israel, the temple was destroyed, and exile and suffering became the mark of their collective condition."[5]

And they see Jesus as a failure because He died: "If he were truly the Messiah he should not have died in the first place!"[6] And so they view Him as "just another martyred Jew who was killed by the Romans for political insurrection."[7]

Yet Daniel 9 predicts exactly these things! Messiah comes and (surprisingly) dies, and Jerusalem does not enter a golden age of peace, but is destroyed by a foreign ruler. Perhaps this was unthinkable, which makes the prophecy even more remarkable.

Of course the rabbi holds his view with good reason. Many prophecies of the Old Testament do speak of Messiah as a king who brings peace to the whole world (see Psalm 72 for just one example). Yet we cannot ignore the many other prophecies that speak of Messiah suffering and dying (see, for example, Isaiah 53). We cannot pretend there is only one kind of prediction. Yet this is not a contradiction, but can fit into a consistent picture: Messiah comes and dies on His first visit, but then comes back later to rule. Even Jesus' disciples had trouble understanding this until He explained it clearly to them: "Wasn't it clearly predicted by the prophets that the Messiah would have to suffer all these things *before* entering his time of glory?" (Luke 24:26, NLT, emphasis supplied). This is what Christians believe about Jesus.

Daniel 9 has been a key text in many Jewish people coming to see Jesus Christ as their Messiah, the rejected king of the Jews. But this remains an extremely sensitive issue with Jewish people. Rabbi Eckstein goes as far as to say, "A Jew who accepts Jesus as Lord or Messiah effectively ceases to be a Jew. He is viewed almost treasonously as having abandoned his faith, given up his Jewish heritage, and severed all links with the Jewish peoplehood. He is like a defector who walked out on his God and his family."[8]

This is understandable, given the tragic history of centuries of "Christian" persecution of Jewish people. And yet the statement is rather harsh on people like Jews for Jesus, many of whom were born into Jewish families and the Jewish faith. They became convinced Jesus is the true Jewish Messiah, although not recognised by most Jews. They would see their new-found faith in Jesus as another step toward God, not a step away. They even claim that faith in Jesus has made them more truly Jewish—as expressed in their T-shirt slogan, "Jesus Made Me Kosher." Such believers see Christianity as fulfilled Judaism.

Other Jewish thinkers find it almost impossible to believe in the idea of Messiah anymore. Dan Cohn-Sherbok, in his book *The Jewish Messiah*,[9] argues that "doctrines connected with the coming of the Messiah . . . have seemed totally implausible," and many Jews "rely on themselves to shape their own destiny." "Instead of looking to a heavenly form of redemption, the Jewish community must now rely on itself for its own survival and the redemption of the world."

Cohn-Sherbok doubts many of the traditional basics of the Jewish faith, arguing that Jews should "free themselves from the absolutes of the past" because "these ancient doctrines can be superseded by a new vision of Jewish life which is human-centred in orientation." He even doubts whether we can even know the truth. For him it is no longer "plausible to assert that any religious outlook is categorically true" and Jews should "recognise that their Scriptures are simply one record among many others" not "possessing truth for all humankind." So after thousands of years of disappointed hopes, he has given up on the idea of a Messiah coming at all, and relaxed almost any claim to religious truth at all. This approach is typical of extremely liberal or agnostic Judaism.

Belief in Jesus is often portrayed as destructive to Judaism, and there is no question many churches have been horrendously anti-Jewish. Peter de Rosa describes churches during the Nazi era that displayed a crucifix with Jesus and the sign "INRI—Jesus of Nazareth, King of the Jews," as well as another sign reading, "Jews are not welcome here." And the crucifix showed Jesus crucified naked—as He really was—but had a loincloth covering up the fact that He was a circumcised Jewish male.[10] Some Christians protested and protected the Jewish people,[11] but in general the churches were silent—or even complicit—during Hitler's holocaust.[12] No wonder Jews are suspicious of Christians.

But Jesus Himself was not anti-Jewish. He was a Jew. He tried His best to save Jerusalem. For example, most people know of His commands to "love your enemies," "turn the other cheek" and "go the second mile." But He was primarily talking about the Roman invaders. A Roman soldier was legally able to make you carry his pack for one mile (or *stadion*). Jesus said it made sense to go two (and this helped keep the Romans onside). When He said to love your enemies, He was also telling Jewish leadership not to be too defiant and annoy the Romans. Rather, Jesus did favours for Romans (see Matthew 8:5-13), trying to model love for one's enemies. Not long after Jesus' death, Jerusalem again defied the Romans—and paid a tragic price. It's staggering that people didn't listen to Jesus or Daniel.

The Jewish leaders objected when the Roman governor Pilate wrote on Jesus' cross, "Jesus of Nazareth, King of the Jews" (see John 19:19-22). But that is exactly what He was.

How do we know Messiah would appear in Jerusalem?

The text has several mentions of Jerusalem. Daniel is told about "your holy city," which—to a Jew—can mean only one place (Daniel 9:24). The rebuilding of Jerusalem is the subject of verse 25 and so, from context, the place where Messiah the Prince will appear. The destruction of the city and its sanctuary (the Jerusalem temple) is the subject of verse 26.

When was Jesus anointed?

"Priests were anointed at 30, and in the year 27 AD Jesus reached that age and was anointed by the Holy Spirit and publicly proclaimed as the Messiah. The New Testament is more specific in dating this event (see Luke 3) than the whole Bible is in regard to any other occasion."[13]

In the Gospel of Luke, we're given dates for the reigns of various rulers, so we can then match these up with Roman historical sources.

"In the 15th year of the reign of Tiberius Caesar—when Pontius Pilate was governor of Judea, Herod tetrarch of Galilee, his brother Philip tetrarch of Iturea and Trachonitis, and Lysanius tetrarch of Abilene—during the priesthood of Annas and Caiaphas, the word of God came to John son of Zechariah in the desert. He went into all the country around the Jordan, preaching a baptism of repentance for the forgiveness of sins" (Luke 3:1-3).

We won't go into all the history of that, but it mentions six historical figures:

- "Tiberius succeeded Augustus in 14 AD, so that the year 28–29 AD is most likely in view. However, the existence of various calendars, lack of knowledge about customs concerning the reckoning of the accession (part-) year, and especially a period of partial coregency with Augustus exclude certainty."[14]
- Pontius "Pilate was prefect of Judea from 26 to 36 AD."[15]
- "Herod Antipas, in accord with the terms of Herod the Great's final will and as confirmed by the emperor Augustus, ruled over Galilee and Perea from 4 BC to 29 AD. Luke mentions only the former territory."[16]
- "Philip was less ambitious than his brothers and received only minor territories. He ruled until his death in 34 AD. Trachonitis is an area south of Damascus. Iturea is a rather fluid designation. A once considerable kingdom centred in Lebanon was gradually carved up into smaller territories."[17]
- "The span of Lysanius' rule is not known. . . . Abilene was immediately west of Damascus."[18]
- "Luke writes 'in the time of the high priest'—but then gives two names, Annas and Caiaphas. This reflects a situation in which Annas, an earlier high priest (6–15 AD) and father-in-law of the current high priest Caiaphas (18–36 AD), retains much of the power and prestige of the high-priestly office (John 18:13, 24; Acts 4:6)."[19]

Analysing this data gives us a possible date range and the year 27 AD fits within this.

A question might occur to you: if history divides around Christ's birth date, why wasn't He born in the year 0? First, there was no year 0. And second, a monk named Dionysius Exiguus (or Denis the Short), who drafted the Gregorian or Western calendar, made a mistake of four years. Thus Christ was actually born in 4 BC—four years *before Christ*, according to Dionysius! But this mistake doesn't affect our chronology.

Did Jesus understand Daniel's prediction?

In His first public speech, Jesus said, "The time is fulfilled, and the kingdom of God is at hand. Repent, and believe in the gospel" (Mark 1:15, NKJV). Jesus elsewhere speaks of Daniel as a prophet and says, "Let the reader understand" (Matthew 24:15). He applied Daniel's predictions to His own era with stunning accuracy.[20]

What did Daniel say Messiah would do?

Earlier in Chapter 9, Daniel has seen Israel's problem: sin. God has great plans for the nation, but people won't cooperate and keep choosing the wrong thing. This sounds typically human. Most of the pain suffered on this planet is due to human "sin," whether large-scale sins like selling drugs and arms for money, or small, private sins like not giving the people closest to us the love they need.

Daniel dreamed of a time when all that would change, and when God's chosen King would start a kingdom where everyone chose love and cooperated with God's plan. That's what Christians call "the kingdom of heaven," when Jesus actually takes over the world and brings massive changes.

The first step to doing that was for God to become human, and to "die for our sins"—that is, to vacuum up all the guilt of all human sin and dispose of it Himself.

The second step is to come back and start a kingdom where everyone has chosen a new way of life by God's plan.

The text describes God's plan "to finish transgression, to put an end to sin, to atone for wickedness, to bring in everlasting righteousness, to seal up vision and prophecy and to anoint the most holy" (Daniel 9:24).

Without going into all the detail, this verse describes God's plan to set up a new kingdom where human sin doesn't wreck everything:

▶ To "finish transgression," and

❱ "Put an end to sin."

These first two terms describe God's willingness to forgive rebellion and sins done purposely (Hebrew *pesha'* meaning wilfully breaking known law) and also accidental sin (*chatta'th* meaning missing the mark).

1. "Atone for wickedness" or sin means Jesus taking the cost and consequences of human guilt (Hebrew *awon* meaning offence, guilt) onto Himself, when He died on the cross. The word *atone* also means to bring reconciliation in a relationship (to make people "at one" again), and it describes the way God and humans are reconciled through what Jesus did.

2. "Bring in everlasting righteousness" (or goodness) suggests a kingdom where humans can live forever without sin or evil.

3. "Seal up the vision and prophecy" means to confirm the accuracy of Daniel's prophetic vision. When we look at it now, we can see convincing evidence that God inspired it, and therefore that God has a plan.

4. "Annoint the most holy" means Jesus acting as a priest to bring reconciliation between humans and God. This is an important topic in the Bible that deserves further study.

For the human heart

This prophecy appeals to our logical mind, but it is more than cold reason. It describes a God who cares about our problems, and has a plan to deal with our failings and guilt, and put our lives back on track—a brilliant feeling.

For those of us who know we are capable of good but also of evil—giving to charity and manipulating our friends in the same day—it tells us God has a plan to help our human condition. God hates sin and the effect it has on us, and He decided to take the problem onto His own shoulders. Christianity teaches that Jesus personally accepted the guilt of sinners like us and paid our debt. Daniel said the Messiah would be "cut off [killed], but not for himself" (Daniel 9:26, NKJV). Jesus died for the human sin problem in a personal sense, for our sin problem.

Jesus died to give us freedom from guilt, and to bring in "everlasting righteousness"—goodness that lasts forever. We know the great feeling inside when we've done the right thing. Imagine having that kind of high permanently. Doesn't that sound like heaven?

Listen to Daniel 9:24-27 personally: Your sin is ended, your guilt is atoned for, the goodness you've been given will last forever. God is not angry with you.

MARY MAGDALENE: WHO WAS SHE?

The key question is how to assemble the jigsaw puzzle of clues left by the Gospel writers: are Mary Magdalene, Mary of Bethany and an unnamed "sinful" woman the same person?

Pope Gregory in 591 AD said yes: "She whom Luke calls the sinful woman, whom John calls Mary [of Bethany], we believe to be the Mary [Magdalene] from whom seven devils were ejected according to Mark."[1] Bible scholar Andre Feuillet agrees,[2] and shows that Gregory was not the first Christian to link the stories: the early Christian writer Tertullian (c 155-220 AD) clearly linked Luke and Matthew, using an idea common to the other two Gospels as well.[3] John Wenham also believes the three women are one and the same, and cites many other 20th century scholars in support.[4]

More importantly, the Gospels themselves contain clues that tend to support this longstanding Christian tradition, and nothing that contradicts it.

Is Mary of Bethany the "sinful woman in that town"?

A careful comparison of the four Gospel stories reveals clues that Mary of Bethany and the "sinful woman in that town" are one and the same person.

The various stories give different details, because their writers have different personalities, varying interests and differing points of view. For example, writers sitting at different places around a dining table would hear and report different details. But their stories would all line up.

But first a word about witness stories. Imagine three people witnessing a car accident. Matthew tells the police, "The Volvo driver was speeding, talking on his phone and not looking when he ran into the back of the Lexus RX350." Mark says, "The silver 4WD braked for a cat and the green car couldn't stop in time." John says, "The blonde in the tennis dress was totally shocked when her SUV was rear-ended by the station wagon."

These stories sound different, but must they necessarily contradict? Not if the male driver of a green Volvo station wagon was speeding and talking on his phone and didn't stop in time when the blonde female, dressed for tennis and driving a silver Lexus four-wheel drive, braked for a cat. The stories can fit perfectly—even though each witness remembered different details and not others. It seems Matthew noticed the cars and the Volvo driver, but not the woman. Perhaps he is interested in cars, but was not in a position to see the woman's face. Mark may be an animal lover who was watching from the footpath ahead of the accident, too far away to see faces. John may be American (from the term SUV) and he noticed the woman first of all. But these individual differences add colour to a story, and are actually marks of truthfulness. The police would welcome the different details because they suggest that the three witnesses had not gotten together to "cook up" their story.

So let's compare the details of the Gospel writers' stories and you can weigh the evidence for yourself. You may want to read the Bible passages first, and then keep these questions in mind: Do all the similarities suggest the same story? Are the differences necessarily contradictions?

At a glance

	MATTHEW 26:6-13	MARK 14:3-9	LUKE 7:36-50	JOHN 12:1-8
1. Town	Bethany	Bethany	–	Bethany
2. Location	House	House	House	House, v 3
3. Timing	Two days before Passover, v 2	Two days before Passover, v 2	–	Jesus *arrived* six days before Passover, v 1
4. Host's name	Simon the leper, v 6	Simon the leper, v 3	Simon the Pharisee, vv 39, 40	–
5. Others present	–	–	–	Martha serves, Lazarus at table
6. Name of woman	Unnamed woman	Unnamed woman	Woman sinner in that town (Bethany), vv 37, 39, 47	Mary of Bethany, sister of Lazarus and Martha, vv 1, 2, cf 11:1, 2

7. Reclining at table	Yes "lie at table"	Yes, v 3 "lie down at table"	Yes "recline at table"	Yes, v 2 "lie at table"
8. Anointed what part of body?	Head, v 7, and body, v 12	Head, v 3	perfume on feet, vv 38, 46	Poured it on Jesus' feet
9. Alabaster jar	Yes	Yes	Yes	(A pint or *litra*)
10. Broke jar	–	Yes	–	–
11. Expensive perfume	Very expensive perfume, v 7	Very expensive perfume, v 3	Perfume, v 38	Expensive perfume, v 3
12. Pure nard	–	Yes, v 3	–	Yes, v 3
13. House filled with perfume	–	–	–	Yes
14. Who voiced objections?	Disciples, v 8	Some of those present, v 4	–	"one of his disciples, Judas," v 4
15. Judas' hidden motive	–	–	–	Thief
16. Indignant	Yes	Yes, 14:4	–	Objected, v 4
17. Why waste?	Yes, v 8	Yes (of perfume)	–	–
18. Should be sold	Yes	Yes	–	Yes
19. Cost	High price	Year's wages (300 denarii)	–	Year's wages (300 denarii)
20. Money to poor	Yes	Yes	–	Yes, v 5
21. Jesus' first comment to defend her	Don't bother her	Leave her alone	–	Leave her alone, v 7
22. JC says she did	What she could	A beautiful thing, v 6, what she could, v 8	(loved much, v 47)	–
23. Poor always	Yes	Yes	–	–
24. Prepare me for burial	Yes, v 12	Yes, v 8	–	Yes, v 7
25. Faith saved you	–	–	Yes, v 50	–
26. Her story will be told wherever the gospel goes	Yes	Yes	–	–

27. Result: Judas plots to betray	Yes, vv 14-16	Yes, v 10	–	Mentioned indirectly, v 4
28. Result: Mary Magdalene travels with Jesus, supports from own finances	–	Yes, but mentioned later: Mark 15:40, 41	Yes. "After this," follows immediately (8:1-3)	–
29. Mary Magdalene demons	–	Yes (16:9)	Yes (8:2)	–
30. Stories right before re: Mary of Bethany	–	–	–	Yes (John 11)

The Simon subplot *(written by Luke from Simon's testimony?)*

a. She stood behind JC	–	–	Yes	–
b. She wet JC's feet with tears	–	–	Yes	–
c. She wiped JC's feet with hair	–	–	Yes	Yes
d. She kissed JC's feet	–	–	Yes	–
e. Simon thinks: if prophet . . .	–	–	Yes	–
f. Jesus reads thoughts			Simon's, v 39	
g. Two debtors story	–	–	Yes	–
h. You gave me no water etc	–	–	Yes	–
i. Sins forgiven, loved	–	–	Yes	–

The stories certainly share a lot of details. On these 39 details, you can find:

- 10 details clearly agreed upon by two writers without contradictions elsewhere (#12, 17, 21, 22, 23, 26, 27, 28, 29, c).
- Six more details agreed upon by three writers without

contradictions elsewhere (#1, 9, 16, 18, 20, 24).

▶ Three more details in all four writers (#2, 7, 11).

▶ 13 details that are mentioned in only one writer, and without contradictions elsewhere (#5, 10, 13, 15, 25, a, b, d, e, f, g, h, i).

▶ Totals:

▶ 32 details without contradiction [5]

▶ Seven differences of detail (#3, 4, 6, 8, 14, 19, 21).

Differences that cannot be "harmonised"—fitted together into a convincing picture—would suggest that the stories describe different incidents.[6] So let's examine them:

#3. Matthew and Mark date the Bethany feast two days before Passover. John says Jesus *arrived* in Bethany six days before Passover—but does not say the feast was held that first day.

#4. Matthew and Mark call the host Simon the leper, while Luke calls him Simon the Pharisee. The name and small town are the same. A leper would never be allowed social contact for fear of contagion, so Simon must have been an ex-leper: Jesus was often recorded as healing lepers (see, for example, Matthew 11:5), and it is likely Simon was one. This could easily be the same Simon from the same place, described to emphasise different details.

#6. Mary of Bethany could well be the "sinner" from Bethany unnamed in the other Gospels. The names are not necessarily contradictory—they could be different names for the same person.

#8. Mary could well have anointed both the head and feet or, speaking more generally, the "body" of Jesus. As shown in chapter 6, anointing the head is fairly typical hospitality, so John may be suggesting head and feet when he writes of "Mary . . . who poured perfume on the Lord [the head would be expected] and wiped his feet with her hair" (John 11:2).[7]

#14. Mark simply records that some people present criticised Mary. Matthew focuses on the disciples, and John is even more specific about which disciple was the ringleader. Perhaps they observed different things from different places around the table.

#19. Two Gospels agree on the price as "a year's wages" or 300 denarii. Matthew does not give the figure but is right to call it a "high price."

#21. Two writers say, "Leave her alone." Matthew says, "Don't bother her." This is the same idea, and Jesus may even have used both lines.

While we are looking at perceived differences, some have argued that Luke's feast story must be different because he puts it earlier in the overall narrative of Jesus. But Luke usually structures his material around an idea, grouping stories around that. Scholars have recognised that he tends to write logically rather than chronologically.[8]

So there are differences, but none that necessarily contradict. Even the precise details can be "harmonised" into a convincing picture.

So arguably Mary of Bethany and the "sinful woman" are one and the same.[9]

Is Mary Magdalene the same person as Mary of Bethany?

This is not obvious in the biblical texts, but there are some intriguing clues and "converging probabilities"[10] that make it plausible.

1. We have already seen that three Gospel writers covered up the identity of a woman with a sinful past, and that John, who was the last to write his Gospel, later revealed her as Mary. This could suggest that the earlier Gospel writers were silent at first about the full story to spare Mary from unwanted publicity[11]—perhaps while she was active in public witness to the truth of Jesus' story. Then her own story could come out later, after her retirement or even her death, and at that time John felt free to name her. Even then, no-one uses the harsh and specific word *prostitute*.[12]

Or perhaps there was a more urgent reason for privacy. Interestingly, the three earliest Gospels do not tell the story of the resurrection of Lazarus of Bethany, the brother of Mary. John later reports a good reason: leading priests were planning to kill Lazarus! (see John 12:9, 10). When the many eyewitnesses to his resurrection spread the story, crowds were flocking to see him and were coming to believe in Jesus, so the priests planned to silence Lazarus permanently. So perhaps the early Gospel writers kept this Bethany family fairly anonymous for security reasons.[13] Calling Mary a

"Magdalene" meant someone from Magdala, a village near Galilee (see Matthew 15:39). This was true if she had lived there, but could also work as a cover story to draw attention from her family home, which was in Bethany, just a short distance from Jerusalem.

This need for privacy could explain why Luke did not name Mary Magdalene as the "sinner," but did name her as a financial supporter of Jesus in the very next chapter (see Luke 8:1-3). Luke could have been wanting to name her good actions and leave her dark past anonymous.

Some would argue that Magdala and Bethany are different towns, and Mary could hardly come from both. Yet she could have lived in both at different times. And prostitution is more likely for a girl living away from her home and family support, and Magdala would be a likely place for prostitution. The rabbis called Magdala a wealthy but morally corrupt town—so much so that they said this was why it was later destroyed. Alfred Edersheim says "its wealth was very great" (largely from producing woollen fabric and dyes taken from shellfish in the lake) but "its moral corruption was also great."[14]

A change of towns could explain why Mary only sometimes has the title Magdalene.[15]

2. Mary Magdalene was "possessed by seven demons" until Jesus exorcised demons from her (see Mark 16:9; Luke 8:2). This hardly fits with the view of Mary as always an upstanding, well-to-do woman, perhaps with a few mildly depressed moments, who financially supported Jesus. "It is understood that demons push people into all manner of sin and vice,"[16] so this could fit well with the idea of Mary Magdalene having a very dark past, morally and spiritually—including sexual sin. A document reflecting similar ideas from around that time, *The Testaments of the Twelve Patriarchs,* lists seven spirits that are sent to humans by "Beliar" (evil or perhaps Satan), and the first is sexual sin ("fornication"). Others listed are gluttony, angry fighting, flattering trickery, arrogance, lying and injustice or theft, and it claims they cause darkening of the mind, not understanding God's law, not obeying parents, and perishing. So demons or spirits were clearly associated with sin in those days. So describing seven spirits could match the comment that Mary of Bethany had "many sins" (see Luke 7:47).[17]

3. Luke seems to suggest Mary Magdalene works and travels with Jesus because of Mary of Bethany's changed life. He shows Jesus telling the "sinner" (Mary of Bethany) that her faith has saved her and she can go in peace. Then his very next scene shows Mary Magdalene serving with Jesus on a mission trip (see Luke 8:1-3), and Luke even suggests that this is the logical result of what went before. English Bibles simply say it happened "After this . . ." (Luke 8:1), but Luke chooses to connect the two scenes with a Greek word "denoting sequence in time, space or logic."[18] We could almost translate, "And so the next thing was. . . ." Wenham writes, "Luke's introduction of Mary Magdalene at the beginning of chapter 8 would be explained if chapter 7 is the story of her conversion."[19]

Luke does not name Mary of Bethany as the woman "sinner" in the anointing story, and he introduces Mary Magdalene almost as if for the first time as Jesus' supporter, but again this could be motivated by a concern for privacy.

4. Mary Magdalene and Mary of Bethany never appear in a scene together.[20]

5. Viewing Mary of Bethany and Mary Magdalene as the same person builds a great story running through the Gospels, and Mary is a consistent personality. Wenham describes her as "impulsive, emotional, devoted, discerning, privileged."[21]

> **(a)** For example, Mary of Bethany appears near her brother's tomb, weeping (the Greek word *klaio* suggests strong weeping and perhaps formal mourning. It is stronger than the word *dakruo*, which means simply to shed tears). Later Mary Magdalene appears near Jesus' tomb, again weeping (*klaio*, compare John 11:31-35; 20:11).[22]

> **(b)** After Jesus' death, Mary Magdalene came to anoint His body for burial (see Mark 16:1, 2). This is the very thing Mary of Bethany was trying to do in the feast at Simon's house, as Jesus recognised and three writers recorded (see Matthew 26:12; Mark 14:8; John 12:7). This would make sense if Mary Magdalene and Mary of Bethany are in fact the same person.

(c) At the feast at Simon's house, Judas assumes that if the perfume were sold, Mary of Bethany would give the money to the poor via the money bag he manages (see John 12:4-6). Why? Because Mary Magdalene was a financial contributor (see Mark 15:40, 41; Luke 8:2). So this suggests Mary of Bethany and Mary Magdalene are the same person.[23]

(d) In what may be merely an artistic hint, Mary is often pictured at Jesus' feet. Mary of Bethany sits at Jesus' feet, listening to Him (Luke 10:39). She falls at His feet to tell Him about the loss of her brother (John 11:32). She anoints His feet (John 12:3). After His resurrection, Mary Magdalene and other women are suddenly met by Jesus: "'Greetings,' he said. They came to him, clasped his feet and worshipped him" (Matthew 28:9). Then, after Mary and the other women told the disciples that He had risen, Jesus appeared surprisingly in the room, and they all held His feet and worshipped Him (Luke 24:39, 40). Perhaps this is because His feet still show wounds from the cross, which prove to them that this is really Jesus, alive again. And so the disciples fall as His feet, in awe that He died for them, and that He rose again. Admittedly, many other people fall at Jesus' feet to ask Him for things or to thank Him (see Matthew 15:30; Mark 5:22; 7:25; Luke 8:41; 17:14), which was a fairly normal practice in that culture (see Matthew 18:29), or sit at His feet to listen to Him (see Luke 8:35). This repeated image could be a literary motif characterising Mary and holding together the various stories.

6. There is only one "other Mary" mentioned in the Gospels. Mary was a common name. Yet in describing the scene near Christ's cross, all four Gospels name only two women named Mary: Mary Magdalene and "the other Mary" (see Matthew 27:61; 28:1). (Jesus' mother Mary was named earlier, but is now identified only by the title "his mother," rather than her personal name.) John says, "Near the cross of Jesus stood his mother, his mother's sister, Mary the wife of Clopas, and Mary Magdalene" (John 19:25). Matthew, Mark and Luke show the same scene and identify "the other Mary" in slightly different words (see table next page), but she is fairly clearly the same person.[24]

Women at the cross and tomb[25]

MATTHEW 27:55, 56	MARK 15:40	LUKE 24:10 (shows the women at the tomb; cf Mark 16:1) AND LUKE 23:49	JOHN 19:25
1 Mary Magdalene	Mary Magdalene	Mary Magdalene	Mary Magdalene
2 Mary, mother of James and Joseph. Later twice called "the other Mary" 27:61; 28:1	Mary, mother of James the younger and Joses. 15:47 also calls her mother of Joses. 16:1 calls her mother of James.	Mary (mother?) of James	Mary the wife of Clopas
3 The mother of the sons of Zebedee	Salome	–	–
4 –	Joanna	– (in Luke 8:3, a woman travelling with Jesus' team)	
5 –	–	–	His mother (name Mary not given, perhaps to avoid confusion of Marys)

Here's the point: Matthew twice mentions "the other Mary" alongside Mary Magdalene (see Matthew 27:61; 28:1). If Mary of Bethany and Mary Magdalene were different people, then there would be two Marys (other than His mother) close to Jesus and prominent in His life story. Then Matthew may have said "one of the other Marys." But he does not, which suggests Mary Magdalene and Mary of Bethany are one and the same Mary.

Each of these points is not conclusive on its own, but taken together can make a case. Mary seems like the same person throughout the story.

Wenham finds it "hard to believe" that this Mary, having been told her beautiful deed would always be remembered, "played no part in the resurrection story, but that the privilege of first seeing the risen Lord was given to another, almost unknown, Mary."[26]

For these reasons Mary Magdalene and Mary of Bethany and the "woman sinner" can be read as the same person, making her story an inspiring example of what the gospel of Jesus does in a human heart. Perhaps this is why Jesus said Mary's story would be told wherever His good news is taught (see Matthew 26:13; Mark 14:9).

REFERENCES

Chapter 1 The cover-up?

1. Dan Brown, *The Da Vinci Code,* page 356.

2. Greg Clarke, *Is It Worth Believing? The Spiritual Challenge of* The Da Vinci Code, Matthias Media, Sydney, 2005, page 46.

3. ibid, pages 37-9.

4. ibid, page 45.

5. ibid, page 46.

6. Brown, op cit, page 332.

7. Michael Green, *The Books the Church Suppressed: Fiction and Truth in* The Da Vinci Code, Monarch Books, Oxford, 2005.

8. Interviewed in Jane Lampman, *Who was Mary Magdalene? The buzz goes mainstream, The Christian Science Monitor online,* 2003.

9. Brown, op cit, page 336.

10. ibid, page 315.

11. ibid.

12. ibid, page 342.

13. ibid, page 336.

14. ibid, page 340.

15. ibid, pages 316-17.

16. See John 4:5, 6; Matthew 4:2; John 11:35, 36; Matthew 4:1; Matthew 13:54-58; Luke 2:52.

17. From the readable treatment of this topic by Norman H Young, "Jesus—Divinity Revealed in Humility," in Bryan W Ball and William G Johnsson (eds), *The Essential Jesus: The Man, His message, His mission,* Pacific Press Publishing Association, Nampa, and Signs Publishing Company, Warburton, 2002, pages 103-23.

18. Brown, op cit, page 317.

19. ibid, page 331.

20. See Bart B Ehrman, *Truth and Fiction in* The Da Vinci Code, Oxford University Press, New York, 2004, pages 36-45, for a discussion of the Hammadi discovery.

21. See James M Robinson, *The Nag Hammadi Library in English,* or www.focus.org.uk/jesus2.htm

22. These documents are available online at <ccat.sas.upenn.edu/~humm/Resources/Texts/nagHam.html> or <www.gnosis.org/naghamm/nhl.html>.

23. For example, the Letters of John.

24. Nicky Gumbel, *The Da Vinci Code: A Response,* Alpha International, London, 2005.

25. Michelle Orecklin, "The Novel That Ate the World," *Time,* April 15, 2005.

Chapter 2 Jesus: Mortal prophet or Son of God?

1. *The Da Vinci Code,* page 315.

2. ibid, page 316.

3. ibid, page 318.

4. Anthony C Thiselton, *The First Epistle to the Corinthians,* pages 29-32, lists a number of scholars whose dates range from 53 to 57, with 54 as most likely.

5. For a discussion of these sources, see Josh McDowell, *He Walked Among Us: Evidence for the Historical Jesus,* Here's Life Publishers, San Bernardino, California, 1988.

6. "Tacitus," *Encyclopaedia Britannica,* 2006 Ultimate Reference Suite DVD, written by Alexander Hugh McDonald, lecturer in Ancient History, Cambridge University.

7. "Lucian," *Encyclopaedia Britannica,* 2006 Ultimate Reference Suite DVD.

8. *The Passing of Perigrinus* 11, 13, www.tertullian.org/rpearse/lucian/peregrinus.htm

9. *Shorter Oxford Dictionary.*

10. Josephus, *Antiquities of the Jews,* 18.3.3. As translated by the Israeli scholar Professor Schlomo Pines from an Arabic manuscript dating to the fourth century. See E M Blaiklock, *Jesus Christ: Man or Myth?* Anzea Books, Sydney, 1983. This quotation has been the subject of much discussion. It seems clear that one variant is a forgery by an early Christian interpolator. However the version we quote has strong manuscript evidence and many commentators, including Professors Blaiklock and F F Bruce, defend its authenticity.

11. Quoted by F F Bruce, *The New Testament Documents: Are They Reliable?* Eerdmans, Grand Rapids, and InterVarsity Press, Downers Grove, 2003, page 114.

12. Some have speculated that *Pandera* was the name of a Roman soldier, allegedly the father of Jesus.

13. Quoted in Ian Wilson, *Jesus: The Evidence,* Weidenfeld & Nicholson, London, 1996, page 39.

14. This list after David N Marshall, "The Risen Jesus," in Bryan W Ball and William G Johnsson (eds), *The Essential Jesus: The Man, His message, His mission,* Pacific Press Publishing Association, Nampa, and Signs Publishing Company, Warburton, 2002, pages 168-91.

15. There has been some discussion as to whether the guard was a Roman guard or a Jewish Temple guard. Josh McDowell argues that the textual evidence suggests a Roman guard and cites Camus and A T Robertson in support of this position. See *The New Evidence That Demands a Verdict,* Thomas Nelson, Nashville, 1999, pages 236-7.

16. For more detailed discussion of the major alternative theories of the Resurrection, see Peter Kreeft and Ronald K Tacelli, *Handbook of Christian Aologetics,* InterVarsity Press, Downers Grove, 1994, pages 176-98; Gary R Habermas and Michael R Licona, *The Case for the Resurrection of Jesus,* Kregel, Grand Rapids, 2004, pages 81-131; and Josh McDowell, *The New Evidence That Demands a Verdict,* Thomas Nelson, Nashville, 1999, pages 257-83.

17. J N D Anderson, Wolfhart Pannenberg and Clark Pinnock, "A Dialogue on Christ's Resurrection," *Christianity Today,* April 12 1968, quoted in McDowell, op cit, 1999, page 258.

18. Quoted in Michael Green, *Man Alive!* InterVarsity Press, Downers Grove, 1968. Cited by Josh McDowell, *Evidence That Demands a Verdict: Historical Evidence for the Christian Faith,* Vol I, Thomas Nelson, Nashville, 1979.

19. See, for example, Mark 14:61-64; John 8:58; 10:25-33; 14:8, 9.

20. Following C S Lewis and Josh McDowell and others.

21. See Matthew 10:8-10. Mark 14:5-7 shows that when He didn't, it was a remarkable exception.

22. Peter Stoner, *Science Speaks,* Moody Press, Chicago, 1963; cited in Josh McDowell, *Evidence That Demands a Verdict: Historical Evidence for the Christian Faith,* Vol I, Thomas Nelson, Nashville,

1979, page 167.

23. *Mere Christianity,* Macmillan, New York, 1952, pages 40-1.

24. C S Lewis, *The Weight of Glory,* Macmillan, New York, 1965, page 92.

Chapter 3 Newton's big apple: Future prophecy

1. *The Da Vinci Code,* pages 312-13.

2. ibid, page 514.

3. ibid, page 431.

4. For example, "The remaining events of Newton's life require little or no comment. In 1705 he was knighted. From this time onwards he devoted much of his leisure to theology, and wrote at great length on prophecies and predictions, subjects which had always been of interest to him."—W W Rouse Ball, *A Short Account of the History of Mathematics,* 4th edition, 1908.

5. historicist.com

6. Isaac Newton, *Observations Upon the Prophecies of Daniel and the Apocalypse of St John,* J Darby and T Browne, London, 1733. See also http://www.historicist.com/newton/title.htm

7. Newton, pages 251-2, cited in Desmond Ford, *Daniel,* Southern Publishing Association, Nashville, 1978, page 51.

8. The respected scholar Tremper Longman III writes, "The book of Daniel sets Daniel in the sixth century BC. There is no doubt or dispute about that. Major figures from this time period, known from other biblical and ancient Near Eastern sources, play an important role in the book. . . . Daniel 1:1 is dated to the third year of the reign of Jehoiakim (605 BC) and the latest references include one to the "first year of King Cyrus" (1:21, 539 BC) as well as to that king's third year (10:1; 537 BC)." Longman acknowledges that a book *set* in the 6th century BC was not necessarily *written* then—many scholars claim Daniel was written or rewritten in the 2nd century, because they see predictions that are uncannily accurate and precise through [until] the second century BC and so assume these must have been written after the event. Longman examines the evidence either way and concludes: "In view of the evidence and in spite of the difficulties, I interpret the book from the conclusion that the prophecies came from the sixth century BC."—*The NIV Application Commentary: Daniel,* Zondervan, Grand Rapids, 1999, pages 21-3.

9. See William H Shea, *Daniel 7–12,* Pacific Press Publishing Association, Boise, 1996, for more details.

10. McDowell also notes, "Daniel knew that the Babylonian captivity was based on violation of the Sabbatic year, and since they were in captivity for 70 years, evidently the Sabbatic year was violated 490 years (Leviticus 26:32-35; II Chronicles 36:21 and Daniel 9:24)."—*Evidence That Demands a Verdict: Historical Evidence for the Christian Faith,* Vol I, Thomas Nelson, Nashville, 1979, page 172.

11. ibid, page 170. With some variation in starting and ending dates, McDowell's overall view of this prophecy is similar to Newton's.

12. Chronologies can vary slightly. For example, Stephen Miller argues for 458 BC and sees Jesus anointed in 26 AD (Stephen R Miller, *Daniel,* Broadman & Holman, 1994, page 266). Josh McDowell says Jesus died in 33 AD (page 173).

13. Daniel chose the Hebrew word *karat,* which suggests violence, and is used in Jewish legal texts of a person condemned to death. It is also the word used to describe making a covenant (usually by killing an animal, see Genesis 15:10, 18; Jeremiah 34:13, 18). "The prophecy thus identifies the Messiah with the sacrifice of the covenant. Like the lamb, His death made possible a covenant and assured divine forgiveness. All this was a language that the Israelites, living in a context where sacrifices were a part of daily life, could easily understand" (Jacques B Doukhan, *Secrets of*

Daniel: Wisdom and Dreams of a Jewish Prince in Exile, Review and Herald Publishing Association, Hagerstown, 2000, pages 148-9).

14. The "flood" is understood this way by Josephus, who watched the event, the Talmud and the great medieval rabbis Rashi, Ibn Ezra and others, writes Jacques Doukhan (page 150).

15. See Walter Kaiser, *The Old Testament Documents,* InterVarsity Press, Leicester, UK, 2001, pages 45-6.

16. "And when he [Alexander] went up into the temple, he offered sacrifice to God, according to the high priest's direction, and magnificently treated both the high priest and the priests. And when the Book of Daniel was showed him wherein Daniel declared that one of the Greeks should destroy the empire of the Persians [another of Daniel's predictions], he supposed that himself was the person intended. And as he was then glad, he dismissed the multitude for the present; but the next day he called them to him, and bid them ask what favours they pleased of him; whereupon the high priest desired that they might enjoy the laws of their forefathers, and might pay no tribute on the seventh year. He granted all they desired" (Flavius Josephus, *Antiquities,* Book XI, Ch viii, 5 (c 330 BC), see www.ccel.org/j/josephus/works/ant-11.htm).

17. See Arthur J Ferch, *Daniel on Solid Ground,* Review and Herald Publishing Association, Washington, DC, 1988.

18. If you would like to explore this prophecy further, see Appendix A.

19. Quoted in Ford, page 198.

Chapter 4 *The Da Vinci Code* and the Bible

1. Brown, *The Da Vinci Code,* pages 312-13.

2. ibid, page 313.

3. ibid.

4. ibid, page 317.

5. ibid.

6. ibid, page 331.

7. See Darrell L Bock, *Breaking the Da Vinci Code,* Nelson, Nashville, 2004, pages 104; and Paul Barnett, *Is the New Testament History?* (Revised Edition), Aquila Press, Sydney South, 2003, page 191.

8. Norman L Geisler, *Baker Encyclopedia of Christian Apologetics,* Baker, Grand Rapids, 1999, pages 532-3, cites Bruce M Metzger, *The Text of the New Testament.*

9. Josh McDowell, *The New Evidence That Demands a Verdict,* Thomas Nelson, Nashville, 1999, page 34, provides a breakdown of the number of surviving manuscripts in ancient language categories.

10. For a discussion of the New Testament manuscripts and their comparison to other ancient literature, see McDowell, ibid, pages 33-8.

11. See McDowell, ibid, pages 38-41, for a discussion of these early manuscripts.

12. See Tacitus, *Annals,* 15.44, and Josephus, *Antiquities,* 18.3.3, who both record that Pontius Pilate (prefect of Judea from 26 to 36 AD) condemned Jesus to death.

13. Geisler, op cit, article "New Testament, dating of," page 528, presents a detailed argument for the early dating of Luke and Acts.

14. Bock, loc cit.

15. Barnett, loc cit.

16. www.earlychristianwritings.com

17. F F Bruce, *The New Testament Documents: Are They Reliable?* (Sixth Edition), InterVarsity Press, Leicester, 1981, page 27.

18. ibid, page 23.

19. ibid, page 25.

20. ibid.

21. See Bart D Ehrman, *Truth and Fiction in* The Da Vinci Code, Oxford University Press, New York, 2004, pages 21-2; Henry Chadwick, *The Penguin History of the Church (Vol 1): The Early Church,* Penguin, London, 1993, page 130; Philip Schaff, *History of the Christian Church (Vol 3): Nicene and Post-Nicene Christianity—From Constantine the Great to Gregory the Great AD 311-590* (Revised Fifth Edition), Hendrickson, Peabody, Massacheusetts, 1889 (reprinted 1996), pages 618-32; Ben Witherington III, *The Gospel Code,* InterVarsity Press, Downers Grove, Illinois, 2004, page 64.

22. Athanasias records 318 at one time, Eusebius notices 250. Schaff suggests they were describing different days.

23. Chadwick, op cit, pages 130-1.

24. See Schaff, op cit, pages 622-30.

25. One exception would be the Jehovah's Witness Bible, a translation that has been called unfairly biased by a wide range of scholars.

Chapter 5 Sex and sexism

1. Brown, *The Da Vinci Code,* page 27.

2. ibid, page 30.

3. ibid, page 414.

4. ibid, page 410.

5. ibid, pages 409-11.

6. ibid, pages 412-13.

7. ibid, page 411.

8. Gordon J Wenham, *Genesis,* Word Books, Waco, 1987, page 84.

9. After Duane A Garrett, *NAC Proverbs, Ecclesiastes, Song of Songs*, Broadman, Nashville, 1993, pages 377-8.

10. H Gollwitzer, *Song of Love: A Biblical Understanding of Sex,* translated K Crim, Fortress, Philadelphia, 1979, page 172; quoted in Garrett, pages 377-8.

11. Barry G Webb, *Five Festal Garments: Christian Reflections on The Song of Songs, Ruth, Lamentations, Ecclesiastes, Esther,* InterVarsity Press, Downers Grove, 2000.

12. See, for example, Elizabeth Huwiler, "The Song of Songs," in Roland E Murphy and E Huwiler, *NIC: Proverbs, Ecclesiastes, Song of Songs,* Hendrickson Publishers, Peabody, Massachusetts, 1999, page 243.

13. Tremper Longman III, *NICOT Song of Songs,* Eerdmans, Cambridge, 2001, page 59.

14. Garrett, op cit, page 378.

15. John Snaith, *NCBC: The Song of Songs,* Eerdmans, Grand Rapids, Michigan, 1993, page 5.

16. Garrett, loc cit.

17. Quoted in Roxanne Roberts, "The Mysteries of Mary Magdalene: *The Da Vinci Code* Resurrects a Debate of Biblical Proportions," *Sunday,* July 20, 2003, page D01.

18. www.danbrown.com

19. Brown, op cit, page 172.

20. This section borrows ideas from www.focus.org.uk/mary4.htm

21. Brown, op cit, page 348.

22. ibid, page 549.

23. ibid, page 593.

Chapter 6 The gospel of Mary

1. Darrell L Bock, *Breaking the Da Vinci Code,* Nelson, Nashville, 2004, page 168.

2. Ben Witherington III, *The Gospel Code,* InterVarsity Press, Downers Grove, 2004, page 20.

3. See the excellent documentary, *The Real Da Vinci Code,* Channel Four, 2004.

4. See Richard Abanes, *The Truth Behind* The Da Vinci Code, pages 45-61, and www.catholic.com/library/cracking_da_vinci_code.asp

5. Brown, *The Da Vinci Code*, page 331.

6. James M Robinson (Editor), *The Nag Hammadi Library in English,* Harper & Row, San Francisco, 1988, quoted in Witherington, pages 87-8.

7. id, "What the Nag Hammadi texts have to tell us about 'liberated' Christianity," in Dan Burnstein (Editor), *Secrets of the Code: The unauthorized guide to the mysteries behind* The Da Vinci Code, CDS Books, New York, 2004, page 99; cited in Clarke, page 105.

8. Bart Ehrman, *Truth and Fiction in* The Da Vince Code, Oxford University Press, New York, 2004, pages 144-5.

9. Brown, op cit, page 330.

10. In interview with Jane Lampman. See Jane Lampman, "Who Was Mary Magdalene? The buzz goes mainstream," www.csmonitor.com/2003/1114/p01s02-ussc.html

11. Lampman, ibid.

12. After John Wenham, *Easter Enigma,* 2nd edition, Baker, Grand Rapids, 1992, pages 22-33. See also A Feuillet, "Les deux onctions faites sur Jesus, et Marie-Madeleine," *RevThom75* (1975), page 361.

13. For example, Mary Ann Getty-Sullivan, *Women in the New Testament,* Liturgical Press, Collegeville, 2001, page 184, puts this down to exaggeration due to the New Testament's "primitive knowledge of the origins of mental and physical illnesses," and says "exorcism aptly represents Jesus' struggle against evils that afflict people in many forms."

14. Michael Wilcock, *The Message of Luke,* InterVarsity Press, Leicester, 1979, page 91.

15. Or an adulterer. We can help define the word *sinner* by the fact that the phrases "tax collectors and sinners" and "tax collectors and prostitutes" seem to be almost interchangeable. (Compare Matthew 9:10, 11 with 21:31, 32.) The phrase in Luke's story is probably "sinner in the city," meaning "public sinner," and the story makes most sense when "'sinner' is understood as a euphemism for 'prostitute' or 'courtesan,'" says John Nolland, *Word Biblical Commentary: Luke 1-9:20,* Word, Dallas, 1989, page 353.

16. In Acts 22:3, being "at the feet of" someone means learning from them.

17. These quotes from John 11.

18. See Donald A Hagner, *WBC Matthew 14-28,* Word, Dallas, 1995.

19. She is a sinner (see Luke 7:37, 39, 47) but Jesus forgives sins (see Luke 7:47, 48, 49). See also Wilcock, op cit.

20. Feuillet, op cit, page 382, cites Legault and Schnackenburg. See John 19:38-42 for the description

of the burial rituals for Jesus' body, performed by Joseph of Arimathea and Nicodemus.

21. Raymond E Brown, *The Gospel According to John I-XII,* Doubleday, New York, 1966, page 454.

22. A M Hunter, *TBC: St Mark,* SCM, London, 1948, page 127; cited in George R Beasley-Murray, *WBC John,* Word Books, Waco, 1987, page 209.

23. Nolland, op cit, page 355.

24. Wilcock, op cit, page 91.

25. The last phrase of Jesus' comment can be translated "as her memorial to me." See Hagner, op cit, page 759.21.

26. F Scott Spencer, *Dancing Girls, Loose Ladies and Women of the Cloth,* Continuum, London, 2004, page 98.

27. ibid, page 95.

28. John Nolland, *Word Biblical Commentary: Luke 18:35–24:53,* Word, Dallas, 1993, pages 1193, 1191.

29. Quoted in Lampman, op cit.

Chapter 7 Right or wrong? Let's make a bet

1. Ashleigh Brilliant.

Appendix A Daniel 9: Digging deeper

1. See William H Shea, *Daniel: A Reader's Guide,* Pacific Press Publishing Association, Nampa, 2005, page 157; see also Desmond Ford, *Daniel,* Southern Publishing Association, Nashville, 1978, pages 229-31.

2. S R Driver, quoted in Stephen R Miller, *Daniel,* Broadman & Holman, 1994, page 258.

3. Jacques B Doukhan, *Secrets of Daniel: Wisdom and Dreams of a Jewish Prince in Exile,* Review and Herald Publishing Association, Hagerstown, 2000, page 145.

4. William H Shea, *Daniel 7–12,* Pacific Press Publishing Association, Boise, 1996, page 55.

5. Yechiel Eckstein, *What Christians Should Know About Jews and Judaism,* page 262.

6. ibid, page 261.

7. ibid, page 262.

8. ibid, page 296.

9. Dan Cohn-Sherbok, *The Jewish Messiah,* T&T Clark, Edinburgh, 1997.

10. Peter de Rosa, *Vicars of Christ,* Corgi, London, 1988, pages 3-6.

11. For example, Dietrich Bonnhoeffer or the Ten Boom family of Holland, see *The Hiding Place* by Corrie Ten Boom and John Scherrill.

12. See, for example, John Cornwell, *Hitler's Pope: The Secret History of Pius XII,* Penguin, London, 1999.

13. Ford, ibid, page 232.

14. John Nolland, *Word Biblical Commentary: Luke 1–9:20,* Word, Dallas, 1989, page 139-40, citing J Finegan, *Handbook of Biblical Chronology,* University Press, Princeton, 1967, pages 259–80; H W Hoehner, *Chronological Aspects of the Life of Christ,* Zondervan, Grand Rapids, 1977, pages 29–44.

15. Nolland. ibid.

16. ibid.

17. ibid, page 140, citing Schurer, *Jewish People*, 1:561–73.

18. ibid.

19. ibid.

20. For discussion of this, see C Mervyn Maxwell, *God Cares*, Vol 2, Pacific Press Publishing Association, Nampa, and Review and Herald Publishing Association, Hagerstown, 1985, pages 13-47.

Appendix B Mary Magdalene: Who was she?

1. In a sermon. A Feuillet, "Les deux onctions faites sur Jesus, et Marie-Madeleine," *RevThom75* (1975), page 361; also David van Biema, "Mary Magdalene: Saint or Sinner?" *Time*, August 11, 2003.

2. Feuillet, ibid. Translated by Eddy Johnson.

3. Tertullian, *De pudicitia, XI, 1, PL2, col 1001B*, writes of "when he permitted the sinful woman to touch his body, washing his feet with tears and drying them with her hair and so with her oil inaugurating his own decease" (from translation by Dr Gösta Claesson, c 1950). Thelwall translates: "He permitted contact even with his own body to the 'woman, a sinner,'—washing, as she did, His feet with tears, and wiping them with her hair, and inaugurating His sepulture with ointment" ("On Modesty," 1870, both available at tertullian.org/works/de_pudicitia.htm). Whichever translation you use, Tertullian links together the "sinner," an idea only in Luke, with getting Jesus ready for burial ("inaugurating his sepulture" or "inaugurating his own decease"), an idea found in all Gospels except Luke. Also, touching Christ's "body" is mentioned only in Matthew. Thus Tertullian brings together the Gospel accounts of this story.

4. John Wenham, *Easter Enigma*, 2nd edition, Baker, Grand Rapids, 1992, page 24, cites A O'Rahilly, *The Family at Bethany*, Cork University Press, Oxford, Blackwell, 1949, page 182, who references 20 "recent" commentators who agree that Mary Magdalene, Mary of Bethany and the sinful woman are the same person.

5. We have chosen conservative figures. For example, #19 is clearly agreed by two writers, but we have not counted this as agreement because another writer offers different detail. Also, our figures would look even more favourable if we included obvious details—for example, that Jesus was there—but we have been conservative.

6. Some scholars assume the traditions have been distorted in transmission. Wenham sees evidence that the Gospel writers were "honest and well informed," and gives them the benefit of the doubt: "The records as they stand are reliable, unless there is compelling reason to the contrary."—Wenham, op cit, page 24.

7. Wenham, op cit, page 25.

8. Feuillet, op cit, page 370.

9. R Holst sees the same incident in all four accounts. "The Anointing of Jesus: Another Application of the Form-Critical Method," *JBL 95* (1976), pages 435-46. Joseph A Fitzmyer finds seven reasons to connect Mark's and Luke's versions, *The Gospel According to Luke 1-9: introduction, translation and notes*, Doubleday, New York, 1981, page 686. C H Dodd sees one incident behind all the accounts, *Historical Tradition in the Fourth Gospel*, Cambridge University Press, Cambridge, 1963, pages 162-73. D A Carson, *The Gospel According to John*, Eerdmans, Apollos, 1991, pages 426-7, disagrees, but observes that some key scholars see mistakes in John due to a false blurring of two accounts: Brown, Marshall, Beasley-Murray. Benoit and Legault see in Luke a different story about another woman. Feuillet sees separate incidents but the same woman, Mary of Bethany = Mary Magdalene = the anonymous sinner.

10. Feuillet's phrase, op cit, page 380.

11. Christopher Wordsworth, *The New Testament of Our Lord and Saviour Jesus Christ in the Original Greek, With Notes and Introductions: The Four Gospels*, Rivingtons, London, 1886, page 323.

REFERENCES

12. Wenham, op cit, page 32.

13. ibid.

14. Jer Taan 69 a; 11 Jer Taan us; Midr on Lament ii 2, ed Warsh page 67 b middle; all in Alfred Edersheim, *The Life and Times of Jesus the Messiah,* Book III, chapter 22, 1883; from http://www.kjvuser.com/lifeandtimes/book322.htm *Migdal* in Hebrew means a tower, so Magdala probably got its name from a defence tower. Several well-known Rabbis came from Magdala and "are spoken of in the Talmud as 'Magdalene' (*Magdelaah,* or *Magdelaya*)." (Baba Mets. 25 a, middle, R, in Edersheim).

15 Wenham, op cit, page 32.

16. Feuillet, op cit, pages 387-8.

17. *The Testaments of the Twelve Patriarchs,* I, 3. It is usually seen as a Jewish document adapted by Christians, and dated approximately 80-200 AD. For an online source, see www.earlychristianwritings.com/patriarchs.html See also Wenham, op cit, page 30.

18. In Luke 8:1, *kathegzes* "denoting sequence in time, space, or logic . . . literally *in the next . . .*" (Friberg); "a sequence of one after another in time, space, or logic" (Louw-Nida).

19. Wenham, op cit, page 28.

20. ibid, page 29.

21. id.

22. F Scott Spencer, *Dancing Girls, Loose Ladies and Women of the Cloth,* Continuum, London, 2004, page 95, and Mary Ann Getty-Sullivan, *Women in the New Testament,* The Liturgical Press, Collegeville, 2001, page 188, point out the parallel between these two verbs and scenes, even though they do not equate the two characters.

23. Feuillet, op cit, pages 384-5, citing A Lemonnyer.

24. ibid, page 381, and see the thorough discussion in Raymond F Brown, *The Gospel According to John, XII-XXI,* Doubleday, New York, 1970, pages 904-6.

25. Following Brown, ibid, page 905.

26. Wenham, op cit, page 29.

FURTHER READING

Richard Abanes, *The Truth Behind* The Da Vinci Code, Harvest House Publishers, Eugene, 2004.

Bryan W Ball and William G Johnsson (eds), *The Essential Jesus: The Man, His message, His mission,* Pacific Press Publishing Association, Nampa, and Signs Publishing Company, Warburton, 2002,

Paul Barnett, *Is the New Testament History?* (Revised Edition), Aquila Press, Sydney South, 2003.

Darrell L Bock, *Breaking the Da Vinci Code,* Nelson, Nashville, 2004.

Sue Bohlin, "The Sacred Feminine and Goddess Worship," www.probe.org

F F Bruce, *The New Testament Documents: Are They Reliable?* (6th Edition), InterVaristy Press, Leicester, 1981.

catholic.com/library/cracking_da_vinci_code.asp

Henry Chadwick, *The Penguin History of the Church (Vol 1): The Early Church,* Penguin, London, 1993.

Paul Copan and Ronald K Tacelli (Editors), *Jesus' Resurrection, Fact or Figment? A Debate Between William Lane Craig and Gerd Ludemann,* InterVarsity Press, Downers Grove, 2000.

Bart D Ehrman, *Truth and Fiction in* The Da Vinci Code, Oxford University Press, New York, 2004.

Arthur Ferch, *Daniel on Solid Ground,* Review and Herald Publishing Association, Washington, DC, 1988.

Desmond Ford, *Daniel,* Southern Publishing Association, Nashville, 1978.

Michael Green, *The Books the Church Suppressed: Fiction and Truth in* The Da Vinci Code, Monarch Books, Oxford, 2005.

Frank B Holbrook (Editor), *70 Weeks, Leviticus, Nature of Prophecy,* Biblical Research Committee, Washington, DC, 1986.

Peter Kreeft and Ronald K Tacelli, *Handbook of Christian Apologetics,* Intervarsity Press, Downers Grove, 1994.

Josh McDowell, *Evidence That Demands a Verdict: Historical Evidence for the Christian Faith,* Vol I, Thomas Nelson, Nashville, 1979.

Josh McDowell, *The New Evidence That Demands a Verdict*, Thomas Nelson, Nashville, 1999.

Stephen R Miller, *Daniel*, Broadman & Holman, 1994.

Brempong Owusu-Antwi, *The Chronology of Daniel 9:24-27*, ATS Publications, Berrien Springs, 1995.

Philip Schaff, *History of the Christian Church (Vol 3): Nicene and Post-Nicene Christianity—From Constantine the Great to Gregory the Great AD 311-590* (Revised 5th edition), Hendrickson, Peabody, 1889 (reprinted 1996).

William H Shea, *Daniel 7–12*, Pacific Press Publishing Association, Boise, 1996.

William H Shea, *Daniel: A Reader's Guide*, Pacific Press Publishing Association, Nampa, 2005.

Ben Witherington III, *The Gospel Code*, InterVarsity Press, Downers Grove, 2004.

www.focus.org.uk/ "Jesus and *The Da Vinci Code*"

AUTHOR NOTE

As co-authors, Grenville Kent and Philip Rodionoff shared ideas and feedback (as they first did in Year 6 History class). The principal contributor to each section is indicated below:

Chapter 1 The cover-up?	GK, PR
Chapter 2 Jesus: Mortal prophet or Son of God?	PR, last section GK
Chapter 3 Newton's big apple: Future prophecy	GK
Chapter 4 *The Da Vinci Code* and the Bible	PR
Chapter 5 Sex and sexism	GK
Chapter 6 The gospel of Mary	GK, first section PR
Chapter 7 Right or wrong? Let's make a bet	GK, PR
Appendix A Daniel 9: Digging deeper	GK
Appendix B Mary Magdalene: Who was she?	GK